AQUATASTIC: SWIMMING MADE SIMPLE

∽

BY: RONDA BRODSKY, M.S.

© Copyright 2007 Ronda Brodsky.
All rights reserved. No part of this publication may be reproduced, stored in a retrieval system, or transmitted, in any form or by any means, electronic, mechanical, photocopying, recording, or otherwise, without the written prior permission of the author.

Note for Librarians: A cataloguing record for this book is available from Library and Archives Canada at www.collectionscanada.ca/amicus/index-e.html
ISBN 1-4251-0783-4

Offices in Canada, USA, Ireland and UK

Book sales for North America and international:
Trafford Publishing, 6E–2333 Government St.,
Victoria, BC V8T 4P4 CANADA
phone 250 383 6864 (toll-free 1 888 232 4444)
fax 250 383 6804; email to orders@trafford.com

Book sales in Europe:
Trafford Publishing (UK) Limited, 9 Park End Street, 2nd Floor
Oxford, UK OX1 1HH UNITED KINGDOM
phone +44 (0)1865 722 113 (local rate 0845 230 9601)
facsimile +44 (0)1865 722 868; info.uk@trafford.com

Order online at:
trafford.com/06-2541

10 9 8 7 6 5 4 3 2

PREFACE

After many years of teaching swimming I thought it was about time for me to write a book. My book entails the proper and innovative techniques that I have used for more than 20 years. This book is meant to be helpful to all Aquatics as well as Physical Education instructors and teachers. Best wishes for an Aquatastic swim.

ACKNOWLEDGEMENTS

I would like to start by thanking everyone at the Aquatic Exercise Association, especially Angie Proctor and Julie See for all of their help, guidance and friendship over the years. I would also like to thank the Jewish Community Center of West Bloomfield, Michigan and Franklin Fitness and Racquet Club of Southfield, Michigan for allowing me the opportunity to gain aquatic experience. I also need to acknowledge and thank the thousands of parents who have allowed me to teach their children to swim. Without all of this and the help and encouragement of my family (especially my parents) and friends, none of this would have been possible. Thank you one and all and I do appreciate everything that has been done to help me succeed.

TABLE OF CONTENTS

Preface 3
Acknowledgements. 5

Chapter 1 Aquatastic: Swimming Made Simple 9
Properties Of Water 11
Learning To Swim – An Introduction. 13

Chapter 2 Aquatic Myths And Facts. 15
Who Is Most Likely To Drown?. 17
Where Do Children Drown? 17
How Do Children Drown? 18

Chapter 3 19

Chapter 4 Motor Development. 28

Chapter 5 The Importance Of Play. 31
Aquatic Games: 33

Chapter 6 36
Aquatastic General Teaching Strategies 40
Teaching 3-5 Year Olds The Aquatastic Way 41
Instruction: Ask Key Questions. 42
Blowing Bubbles For The Real Beginners:. 42
Learning To Float:. 43
Opening Eyes Under Water:. 43
Kicking And Floating On The Back: 44
What You Need To Go Swimming: Basic Swimming Gear 44
Swimming Strokes 45
Common Features Of Swimming Strokes 46
Freestyle Or Front Crawl 46
Back Crawl – Backstroke 48
Breast Stroke 48
Side Stroke 50
Butterfly 51
Swimming Under The Water 52
Entries And Exits Into The Water In The Aquatastic Environment:. 53

Chapter 7 General Water Safety Tips **56**
General Safety Considerations. *63*
Risk Management *64*
Guide To Safety Tips In The Aquatic Environment *65*
Exposure Control Plan. *71*
Exposure Determnation Of Job Classifications: *74*

Chapter 8 Adapted Aquatics **78**

Chapter 9 . . . . **86**
Elements Of Successful Instruction *87*
Getting Ready To Teach: Safety Of Your Students:. *88*
Presenting Your Teaching Material:. *88*
Teaching Methods:. *89*

Ronda Brodsky's Biography *90*
References and Bibliography. *91*

Chapter 1

AQUATASTIC: SWIMMING MADE SIMPLE

Children are usually fascinated and curious by the water and this can be and usually is a very dangerous situation. Even if this individual knows how to swim it can be dangerous situation unless safety is stressed in great detail. Teaching children to swim must be done in progression while maintaining safety in the aquatic environment. No matter what your age or swimming ability, you can always be made safer near and in the aquatic environment. Learning to swim is vital, but you must know how to prevent the risk of drowning even before you and especially your children know how to swim.

Many children have the ability to swim before they can walk. Children from the age of 6 months and on have the ability to swim or least the ability to learn the basic swimming techniques. Swimming, similar to any other sport, needs to be practiced on a regular basis. Swimming can be seen as a creative art, is also on-going learning process and it needs to be re-taught and re-enforced continually. Swimming the Aquatastic way is a gradual learning process based on practice, developmental levels, re-enforcement, and the laws of physics.

While some people drown when participating in some form or aquatic activity, many of these people do not intend to be in the water at that time. In many cases these people have accidentally fallen in the water. Drowning can occur anywhere, even in as little water as one inch. That is why we must take all the necessary precautions that we can to prevent drowning.

Pool side and other swimming related accidents are the second leading cause of death for children under the age of 14. The majority of those who drown are clothed and do not intend to enter the water and they are also usually within a few feet of safety. The pool is a very dangerous place as drowning can occur pool side or on aquatic apparatuses such as diving boards. Each year approximately 1,000 children die in aquatic related accidents and over 5,000 others are hospitalized. In addition to that, spas and Jacuzzis also kill over 200 children annually. Adults see themselves as safe as they believe they know more but they are not immune from aquatic accidents. Most adults suffer sever injuries when they combine alcohol and swimming or they over estimate their ability in the aquatic environment. Severe spinal injuries may result when diving into water that is too shallow.

AQUATASTIC: SWIMMING MADE SIMPLE   *Ronda Brodsky*

> *Statistics were taken from* <u>The American Academy of Pediatrics Policy statement on Drowning in infants, Children and Adolescents (RE9319)</u> *and the* <u>Center for Disease Control Statistics on Unintentional Drownings</u>

Aquatastic: Swimming Made Simple is intended to help instructors learn how to teach swimming and/or improve their skills as an aquatic instructor. This book is written in an easy to read format with terms that every individual can understand. It is based on 20 years of experience in the aquatics field. It is written in attempts to help our nation decrease the drowning levels. There is a tremendous need for people of all ages to be safe in and around the aquatic environment as the rates of drowning are increasing at too high of a rate

Most statistics have demonstrated that we constantly need to move with our young children. We need to prevent these young children from being another statistic. Statistics show that children under the age of 6 are at greater risk of death by drowning than any other age group except for young adults. Most drowning of young children occurs in unsupervised aquatic environments involving bathtubs, backyard pools and hot tubs. Parents need to be reminded that even if a child can move and use locomotor skills in the water, they still lack the judgment to recognize dangerous situations and the ability to swim to safety if needed. You should never swim alone and every safety precaution must be taken in and around the Aquatastic environment.

Drowning can occur very quickly. Water depth can be as little as an inch of water. Many of these drownings happen when the child is left alone or unsupervised, even for a brief moment in time. Taking the time to answer a phone call or the door bell could be too long to leave any child unsupervised and/or alone. Many or most of these children are unfortunately forgotten about and not found or remembered about until about 10 minutes after they have been left alone. Many of these drownings are left in the hands of the parents and they fail to keep a close eye on the child in or around the aquatic environment.

Water is an excellent medium for all individuals. Aquatics have many benefits. Here are the main ones:

- Increase muscle strength and endurance
- Increase balance and coordination
- Increase in ease of joint mobility and range of motion
- Decrease pain levels in the joints

Enhancing the individuals self image should be highly stressed in the aquatic environment. Being successful in any endeavor enhances the individuals self image and the success available through aquatics is vital. Success increases the individuals regard for his or her worth and abilities, and it can also decrease the emotional impact of the individual. The water can also be used as an emotional outlet as it may be slapped, pushed, splashed and kicked and this may be how some individuals vent their energies and frustrations. The aquatic environment is one in which anyone can release his or her frustrations in a safe manner.

Water is the high tech tool of our time. Immersion in the water is dependent upon the condition of the participant and his or her fears in the water. Total immersion, which is about 80 percent of the body under water, is usually accomplished, and even more when the person is comfortable and learns how to swim. People are fascinated by water. Its colors soothe, its sounds pacify and it temporarily liberates us from the tyranny of gravity (which could be noted as the most important) effects us all. It translates into compliance for most of us and lifelong habits for the rest of us.

This manual provides information and teaching suggestions to help you plan and conduct aquatic and or swimming sessions while effectively maintaining the highest professional standards available. Before beginning any program, it is recommended that you familiarize yourself with your environment and how things are maintained in that area. The goal here is to provide the safest and best program that you can.

The key to the Aquatastic environment is fun. Having fun and enjoying what you are doing are a vital component and force to learning. The goal and focus here is safety as there is no real way of drown-proofing anyone. The whole Aquatastic philosophy is based upon enjoyment while learning how to swim in a positive and fun environment where you want to be. While having fun the student will gain trust and comfort with you, the instructor. It is now time to read on and enjoy the Aquatastic truth.

PROPERTIES OF WATER

LOOKING at water, you might think that it is the simplest thing around. Pure water is colorless, odorless, and tasteless. But it is not at all simple and plain and it is vital for all life on Earth. Where there is water there is life, and where water is scarce, life has to struggle or just "throw in the towel."

What is water? According to Mirriam Webster water is a major constituent of all living matter and that when pure is an odorless, tasteless, very slightly compressible liquid oxide of hydrogen H_2O which appears bluish in thick layers, freezes at 0° C and boils at 100° C, has a maximum density at 4° C and a high specific heat, is feebly ionized to hydrogen and hydroxyl ions. Water is the only chemical that we know of on earth that occurs naturally in three different physical states of matter: solid, liquid and gas.

We live on a planet that is dominated by water. More than 70 percent of the Earth's surface is covered with it. Water is also essential for life. Water is the major constituent of almost all life forms. Most animals and plants contain more than 60 % water by volume. Without water life would probably never have developed on our planet. About 70% of the human body is water. More than half of the world's animal and plant species live in the water. The human body needs 2 liters of water a day in our climate; we can last only a few days without water. Most of our food is water: tomatoes (95%), spinach (91%), milk (90%), apples (85%), potatoes (80%), beef (61%), and hot dogs (56%).

AQUATASTIC: SWIMMING MADE SIMPLE *Ronda Brodsky*

There are a few physical laws governing our bodies while in water. The main principle involved in the water is that of buoyancy. Archimedes' Law states that a body submerged in a liquid such as water, is buoyed up by a force equal to that of the liquid that displaces it. If we apply this law to Aquatastic, the upward force that acts on the swimmer is equal to the weight of the volume of water that is identical with the volume of the submerged portion of the swimmer's body. The main factor determining buoyancy factors is that of the ratio between weight and volume. Other factors can influence these buoyancy factors, as the swimmer becomes more proficient in the water. Breath control, balanced center of gravity, relaxation, and knowledge of the perfection of the skill are those factors affecting the proficiency in the water.

When in water, some objects will float while others will sink. And some objects will neither sink nor float. These are all functions of buoyancy. If an object floats it is known to have positive buoyancy. While an object that sinks is known as negatively buoyant. Any object that neither sinks nor floats is known as neutrally buoyant. Archimedes, a Greek mathematician put a name on this theory of buoyancy. The Archimedes Principle states: Any object, wholly or partially immersed in a fluid, is buoyed up by a force equal to the weight of the fluid displaced by the object. From this principle we can hopefully sum up that objects in fluid are based on the weight of the object in addition to the amount of water that the object displaces. Archimedes Principle can be applied to any fluid, and as swimmers we need to understand this concept in order to understand how people float and/or sink in the water.

This buoyancy factor is usually the first one felt by the swimmer, as it hits you as you enter the pool. When the body displaces a weight of water that is greater that its own weight it will tend to float and not sink. The degree of buoyancy will greatly depend upon the person's body type. Bone and muscle have a greater mass of gravity than does fat tissue. Looking at this would explain why people with higher muscle mass tend to have a higher rate of gravity which would result in negative gravity. Negative gravity results in the body's tendency to sink in the water.

On land our bodies rotate around the center of gravity, which is usually around the hip. In the water, the body does the same but the center of gravity in the water tends to be around the chest. Reason being is that the lungs in the chest region fill with air and make them lighter and this will make it the most buoyant part of the body.

Sir Isaac Newton (1642-1727) worked extensively in the areas of gravity and the laws of motion, but he was recognized as an English mathematician and philosopher. Understandings of Newton's three laws of motion apply to humans while in the aquatic environment. If we truly understand Newton's principles then and only then can we go on in our study of Aquatastics and learn to be a proficient swimmer.

The first law is the law of inertia. The law of inertia states that a body remains at rest or in uniform motion unless acted upon by a force. The second law is the law of acceleration. The reaction of the body as measured by its acceleration is proportional to the force applied and inversely proportional to the mass. The third law is that of action and reaction. For every action there is an equal and opposite reaction.

Application of the law of inertia to swimming means that there are two types of inertia involved: resting or stationary inertia; and inertia that is moving. If the body is moving it will tend to keep moving and if the body is resting or stationary then it will tend to stay that way until the body is moved. Acceleration states that a body is proportional to the force applied to it and that is the direction in which the body will move. The law of acceleration has to do with the relationship between a force, a push or a pull, and changes in motion. In the third law, you can see this by a swimmer moving forward as he or she moves the water backward. Force can be defined as anything that tends to change the motion of things. A torque is when a force tends to change the state of rotation of things, because of the way it is applied to the body. To make a body move in the aquatic environment you must apply force. To make a body part turn in the aquatic environment you must apply torque.

The Law or Readiness. This law takes affect when someone is ready to act in a certain way. It is the ability to act in a way that is not annoying to others. Students must be ready to learn both physically and mentally if they want to achieve their goals. Readiness can only be achieved if the person is able to successfully function in that activity. This readiness can be developed through motor skills, strength of the individual and through the mental maturity of that individual. Readiness will be best experienced and achieved when the student can experience success.

LEARNING TO SWIM – AN INTRODUCTION

As educators and as parents we tend to rely on the saying that "practice makes perfect." But we must remember that it is proper practice that will make it perfect. We need to enforce doing things over and over again but they must be practiced correctly and efficiently. We need to focus on the activity being done with the student and make sure they are improving and not practicing incorrect techniques. Too often we take this statement for granted and just assume that people will improve if they just practice. And in many cases this lack of success or achievement will de-motivate the student and make him or her less apt to continue what they were practicing. In other cases the student is becoming fatigued too quickly and the skill level continues to decelerate. The principle of frequency must also be looked at while practicing. Practice needs to be stressed as an important factor in learning any skill.

The frequent repetition of any movement involving the same nerve and muscle activity over and over again, will establish the moving pattern. The greater the repetition is and the more firmly it is established the greater the movement pattern should be. If the movement is not appropriate due to their current age or ability, they will not achieve the knowledge of the correct movement pattern. We need to focus on practicing the correct movement because if it is not corrected early enough, then the wrong pattern could be the permanent pattern for any particular movement. Most individuals will adapt and opt for movements that they have success in and by doing this they will learn how to cope better. Success must be planned and practiced in order to fully achieve one's goal.

These opportunities for success are expected as part of the teacher's role. This learning experience should be structured so the knowledgeable teacher understands the role of how students learn and progress in life. Through their knowledge of children, they can use these learning experiences to teach the more technical aspects of swimming to children. The teacher should plan, observe, communicate and organize these goals in order to offer the students a structured and attainable swimming session. This session should offer the students plenty of chances for successes and improvements. The teacher should be able to plan the class according to the specific needs of the students in each course. Each step should be small and build on one another as they will all be in progressive order from easiest to hardest. Only a small change or addition should be needed in order for the student to achieve success

Chapter 2

AQUATIC MYTHS AND FACTS

- **You need to wait 30 minutes after eating to go swimming.**
This is a fallacy and it will all depend on what you eat. If you are doing strenuous swimming then you may want to wait as it may lead to muscle cramps and increased risk for drowning as you may be more fatigued. The main reason that people believe in this rule is that if children do eat a lot before they go swimming they may have an increased chance of vomiting especially if they are very active in the pool. Using common sense in this manner will best help you judge when it is safe for you to go in the water.
- **Children can be drown proofed.**
Regardless of age or swimming ability no one can ever be drown proofed. You may have excellent swimming skills and know the aquatic environment but there may always be something that is unknown in the aquatic environment. You may be in unfamiliar waters or you may unexpectedly get sick in the water. This is also the reason that you should never swim alone.
- **Children under that age of 3 cannot really learn to swim.**
Swimming is a voluntary locomotion through the water. As long as the skills are taught developmentally and age appropriate, children can learn to swim at any age. The key here is confidence and age appropriate but the child must never be left alone even in the bathtub as he or she can drown in an inch of water.
- **Swimming causes ear infections.**
A child's Eustachian tube is generally shorter from the middle ear. This can and will prevent the exchange of fluids when the mucous membranes are swollen which may be due to congestion. Swimming may leave water in the child's ear and all you really need to do is dry the water out of the child's ear. You can buy over the counter swimmers ear drops or you can use a mixture of hydrogen peroxide and vinegar. All you need to do is to remember to get the water out and while the child is swimming you can remind him or her to tilt the head to each side to get water

out of the ears. A child can just as easily get an ear infection if he or she gets water in the ears from the shower.
- **Children cannot learn to swim with tubes in his or her ear.**

This will all depend on the physician and the severity of the child's condition. Deep submersion may not be recommended but they can get their ears wet in most cases. Many physicians ask that the child wears some kind of ear protection in the water to help the child prevent the water from getting into the ear. Always check with the physician and follow his or her orders.
- **Children's swimming lessons should be all work and no play.**

A child's job is to play. A child needs guidance through learning instead of lectures and a more rigid environment. The lesson should be structured but the children need to learn in a more guided environment. Swimming should be FUNdamental and they should learn while playing and most of the time the child will not realize he or she is learning to swim.
- **Children should always wear flotation devices.**

A child needs to learn to float by trusting his or her own body. Flotation devices also provide parents a mistaken notion that the child can be left alone and that he or she will be ok. The flotation devices distract the parent or caregiver from the constant vigilance around the aquatic environment. This includes water wings. Water wings keep children upright but do not rely on them as they restrict arm movement and they encourage the wrong and improper method or position for swimming.
- **Children contaminate pools and throw off the chemical balance of the water.**

If the pool is properly maintained the child should not affect anything. If the pool is properly maintained the transmission of disease will not be present. Most diseases are transmitted person to person and not from pools or the aquatic environment. Proper chlorine levels will prevent disease transmission.
- **Toys and equipment are unnecessary distractions for children during swimming lessons.**

These items offer valuable sources of distraction such as fear of the water. Toys and equipment encourage play and also encourage new ways for the child to move in the water. The toys set up a good background and a solid foundation for the child to learn.
- **You cannot learn to swim unless you know the proper mechanics.**

Confidence in yourself and your ability will allow you to learn to swim. The mechanics of swimming will come as you become more confident in yourself and your aquatic ability. You need to learn how to become confident in order to try and prevent panicking. You must overcome any fears and become confident in yourself before you can really learn to swim. Being in control of yourself and your environment will make you safe and then you can properly learn to swim.

- **I will never be a good swimmer as I am a sinker.**

It is a well known fact that body fat weighs less than muscle and it will help you float. Body fat is rarely seen as an asset when swimming as sinkers have a lower body fat percentage. Sinkers tend to have a greater muscle mass which will lead them to sink more. These individuals can learn to swim but it may take more effort. It all seen as mind over matter. You can do it if you believe in yourself and in your aquatic abilities.

This is only a partial list of what I believe are swimming myths. I am sure there are many more that you have heard of but this is what I usually hear when I teach swimming. There is still a great amount of research that needs to be done in the aquatic field and that is why can only give you what I know. Many of these are my beliefs but some are backed by current research, so now it is your turn to do some research and find out all you can about aquatics.

WHO IS MOST LIKELY TO DROWN?

Children – drowning is the 2nd leading cause of injury-related death for children aged 1-14 years, accounting for 940 deaths in 1998.

- Males – drowning rates were at least 3 times greater for males than for females. In 1998, males comprised 81% of people who drowned in the United States.
- Blacks – the overall age-adjusted drowning rate for black children was 42.6% higher for blacks than for whites. Black children ages 5 through 19 years drowned at 2.5 times the national average.

WHERE DO CHILDREN DROWN?

Residential swimming pools account for 60-90% of drownings for children aged 0-4 years. Half of these drownings occur at the child's own home.

Children who drown in residential pools had been:

- last seen inside their home;
- gone for less than 5 minutes; and
- in the care of either or both parents at the time.

Young children (as well as adults) don't splash, struggle or make noise when in danger in water, and often quickly drown in silence.

HOW DO CHILDREN DROWN?

How young children drown depends on their age.

Children younger than 1 year often drown in:
- toilets
- buckets
- 5-gallon industrial containers or bathtubs

Children aged 1-4 are most likely to drown in hot tubs, spas and swimming pools.

Children aged 5-14 most often drown in swimming pools and open water such as rivers, lakes, dams and canals.

Chapter 3

Child development is the pattern of change that occurs as children grow from birth to adolescence. The study of child development includes descriptions of how, when, why and in what order changes occur. When you understand what a child's capabilities should typically be at different age levels, you know what to expect from the child. You will also notice if a child is developmentally ahead and may need some extra challenges. You should also notice when something is not right.

In order to study and teach children effectively, researchers generally look at specific areas of development. Child development is often broken down into these areas of development: physical, intellectual, emotional, social and moral.

Physical development includes the growth of the body as well as its abilities. Growth in height and weight are usually a very obvious aspect of physical development. Growth is most dramatic during infancy and adolescence. As children develop physically, they gain new abilities. Those abilities will depend on the use and control of the muscles, a study called motor skills or development. Coordination and balance accompany physical development. Learning these skills can pose many challenges for children. Children will experience coordination and balance over and over again as they try out new physical skills and work toward the mastering of these skills.

Intellectual development, which is also known as cognitive development, will occur as children learn to think, understand, reason and use language. This is the area where children will learn to use their brain to the fullest potential. The learning process here is still not completely understood as it is very vast and contains many areas. Research has helped by allowing us to gain knowledge about how this area of development should take place. We enter the world as ready and eager individuals relying a tremendous amount on our senses. We utilize our senses - sight, taste, smell, hearing and touch in almost everything we do. Our early years of development bring numerous and rapid growth opportunities in a child's way of thinking. Complex challenges increase our intellectual capabilities gradually as wee continue to grow and develop. Eventually these skills should lead us to learning how to analyze, how to evaluate things and how to solve problems.

Emotions are feelings about ourselves, others and about the world around us. As we develop emotionally these feelings are expressed and some of them are positive or good feelings while others are negative or bad feelings. Everyone at some time or another will experience both positive and negative emotions. Children hopefully experience more positive than negative emotions and this will help them attain a positive self image. Children who experience these positive emotions tend to be emotionally well adjusted. We all understand and know that part of living means that we will experience some negative emotions, and if they are managed properly we will have nothing to worry about. Negative emotions are at times normal and expected under certain situations, such as crying at a funeral or losing a loved one. Children need to learn how to handle emotions appropriately and if they are negative emotions they need to learn how to recover and accept those emotions. Positive and rewarding emotional development heavily depends on the treatment a child receives. Children will need to learn affection when they receive affection, and they will need to learn to treat others well when they are treated well. Emotional development is very complex but it has a great impact on a child's development.

Social development occurs when children learn how to relate to other people. They learn the skills they need to get along with people and how they can positively fit into society. Children will learn how to share, trade and how to play together. The will learn how to settle fights (some better than others) by using words, rather than just by fighting back. As children develop socially they will learn that society has numerous rules to live by. If social development occurs positively it will serve children well in getting along in society. Without proper social development individuals may feel isolated, alone and not accepted by society.

Lastly we have the area of moral development which is the study of right and wrong. Our values are our beliefs and attitudes about what is important to us. Moral development cannot occur until children learn what is right and wrong. Families, among religion and society can teach many values. Anything children learn will have social impact as it will affect how they interact with other people.

To truly understand how development in children works, you will need to be aware of certain principles. All development is interrelated. All areas of development will inevitably influence another area of development in some way. You can study each area separately but in real life they cannot be separated. Development will follow a similar pattern for children of all ages. Regardless of the child's background or ability level, it will still follow the same pattern. Children all over the world will still follow these same patterns. There are many interesting things about the way a child develops, with the most exciting part being that it does not occur at exactly the same rate for every child. Each child is unique and therefore, will experience new abilities at his or her own rate. Averages of abilities and skills to be learned are noted but they do not necessarily mean that all children will develop that ability at the same time. Therefore, an average age will give you some general information but it will not be exact.

As someone dealing with children, we must be careful not to compare children. Children who develop quicker should be noted as superior unlike their counterparts who should not be labeled as inferior. We must look at the abilities of all children and not the disabilities of all children. Every child is unique and special and we must make them feel that way in our classes. Comparing children can make them feel uncomfortable or inadequate and it will only lead to trouble and problems in the future.

Development in children is ongoing and it does not stop at a certain age. It is more noticeable at earlier ages, but it is a continual process throughout life. As we get older the development is called life span development and not child development and we are no longer children. This is the complete package in development and we can help children set standards for development at a later stage in life. Children need positive influences and encouragement as they go through the different stages and aspects of development.

Development is also seen as sequential, which means that it follows a logical sequence or order. The main sequences of development are from top to bottom and from center to outside. Cephalocaudal development is another name for top to bottom development. This means that children will progressively master all body movements and all of their coordination beginning at the head and working their way down the body. Proximal distal development tends to develop from the center of the body and outward toward the hands and feet. An example of this would be the ease of moving the shoulders compared to using fine motor skills with the fingers. The areas of development will also occur from the large to the small. This means a child will be able to walk before he or she can throw or catch a ball. The last phase of sequential development is that of general to specific. All abilities will start out very simply gradually gaining more and becoming more complex. You need to start with the beginning in order to achieve the end.

AQUATASTIC: SWIMMING MADE SIMPLE   *Ronda Brodsky*

Physical and Language	Emotional	Social
Birth to 1 month: Feedings: 5-8 per day Sleep: 20 hrs per day Sensory Capacities: makes basic distinctions in vision, hearing, smelling, tasting, touch, temperature, and perception of pain	Generalized Tension	Helpless Asocial Fed by mother
2 to 3 months Sensory Capacities: color perception, visual exploration, oral exploration. Sounds: cries, coos, grunts Motor Ability: control of eye muscles, lifts head when on stomach.	Delight Distress Smiles at a Face	Visually fixates at a face, smiles at a face, may be soothed by rocking.
4 to 6 months Sensory Capacities: localizes sounds Sounds: babbling, makes most vowels and about half of the consonants Feedings: 3-5 per day Motor Ability: control of head and arm movements, purposive grasping, rolls over.	Enjoys being cuddled	Recognizes his mother. Distinguishes between familiar persons and strangers, no longer smiles indiscriminately. Expects feeding, dressing, and bathing.
7 to 9 months Motor Ability: control of trunk and hands, sits without support, crawls about.	Specific emotional attachment to mother. Protests separation from mother.	Enjoys "peek-a-boo"

10 to 12 months Motor Ability: control of legs and feet, stands, creeps, apposition of thumb and fore-finger. Language: says one or two words, imitates sounds, responds to simple commands. Feedings: 3 meals, 2 snacks Sleep: 12 hours, 2 naps	Anger Affection Fear of strangers Curiosity, exploration	Responsive to own name. Wave bye-bye. Plays pat-a-cake, understands "no-no!" Gives and takes objects.
1 to 1 ½ years Motor Ability: creeps up stairs, walks (10-20 min), makes lines on paper with crayon.	Dependent Behavior Very upset when separated from mother Fear of Bath	Obeys limited commands. Repeats a few words. Interested in his mirror image. Feeds himself.
1 ½ to 2 years Motor Ability: runs, kicks a ball, builds 6 cube tower (2yrs) Capable of bowel and bladder control. Language: vocabulary of more than 200 words Sleep: 12 hours at night, 1-2 hr nap	Temper tantrums (1-3yrs) Resentment of new baby	Does opposite of what he is told (18 months).
2 to 3 years Motor Ability: jumps off a step, rides a tricycle, uses crayons, builds a 9-10 cube tower. Language: starts to use short sentences controls and explores world with language, stuttering may appear briefly.	Fear of separation Negativistic (2 ½ yrs) Violent emotions, anger Differentiates facial expressions of anger, sorrow, and joy. Sense of humor (Plays tricks)	Talks, uses "I" "me" "you" Copies parents' actions. Dependent, clinging, possessive about toys, enjoys playing alongside another child. Negativism (2 ½ yrs). Resists parental demands. Gives orders. Rigid insistence on sameness of routine. Inability to make decisions.

3 to 4 years Motor Ability: Stands on one leg, jumps up and down, draws a circle and a cross (4 yrs) Self-sufficient in many routines of home life.	Affectionate toward parents. Pleasure in genital manipulation Romantic attachment to parent of opposite sex (3 to 5 yrs) Jealousy of same-sex parent. Imaginary fears of dark, injury, etc. (3 to 5 years)	Likes to share, uses "we" Cooperative play with other children, nursery school. Imitates parents. Beginning of identification with same-sex parent, practices sex-role activities. Intense curiosity & interest in other children's bodies. Imaginary friend.
4 to 5 years Motor ability: mature motor control, skips, broad jumps, dresses himself, copies a square and a triangle. Language: talks clearly, uses adult speech sounds, has mastered basic grammar, relates a story, knows over 2,000 words (5 yrs)	Responsibility and guild Feels pride in accomplishment	Prefers to play with other children, becomes competitive prefers sex-appropriate ac

Physical Development Walks well, goes up and down steps alone, runs, seats self on chair, becoming independent in toileting, uses spoon and fork, imitates circular stroke, turns pages singly, kicks ball, attempts to dress self, builds tower of six cubes. **Emotional Development** Very Self-centered, just beginning a sense of personal identity and belongings, possessive, often negative, often frustrated, no ability to choose between alternatives, enjoys physical affection, resistive to change, becoming independent, more responsive to humor and distraction than discipline or reason.	**AGE 2**	Social Development Solitary play, dependent on adult guidance, plays with dolls, refers to self by name, socially very immature, little concept of others as "people." May respond to simple direction. Intellectual Development Says words, phrases and simple sentences, 272 words, understands simple directions, identifies simple pictures, likes to look at books, short attention span, avoids simple hazards, can do simple form board.
Physical Development Runs well, marches, stands on one foot briefly, rides tricycle, imitates cross, feeds self well, puts on shoes and stockings, unbuttons and buttons, build tower of 10 cubes. Pours from pitcher. **Emotional Development** Likes to conform, easy going attitude, not so resistive to change, more secure, greater sense of personal identity, beginning to be adventuresome, enjoys music.	**AGE 3**	**Social Development** Parallel play, enjoys being by others, takes turns, knows if he is a boy or girl, enjoys brief group activities requiring no skill, likes to "help" in small ways--responds to verbal guidance. **Intellectual Development** Says short sentences, 896 words, great growth in communication, tells simple stories, uses words as tools of thought, wants to understand environment, answers questions, imaginative, may recite few nursery rhymes

Physical Development Skips on one foot, draws "Man", cuts with scissors (not well), can wash and dry face, dress self except ties, standing broad jump, throws ball overhand, high motor drive. **Emotional Development** Seems sure of himself, out-of bounds behavior, often negative, may be defiant, seems to be testing himself out, needs controlled freedom.	**AGE 4**	**Social Development** Cooperative play, enjoys other children's company, highly social, may play loosely organized group games - tag, duck-duck-goose, talkative, versatile. **Intellectual Development** Uses complete sentences, 1540 words, asks endless questions, learning to generalize, highly imaginative, dramatic, can draw recognizable simple objects.
Physical Development Hops and skips, dresses without help, good balance and smoother muscle action, skates, rides wagon and scooter, prints simple letters, handedness established, ties shoes, girls small muscle development about 1 year ahead of boys. **Emotional Development** Self-assured, stable, well-adjusted, home-centered, likes to associate with mother, capable, of some self-criticism, enjoys responsibility. Likes to follow the rules.	**AGE 5**	**Social Development** Highly cooperative play, has special "friends", highly organized, enjoys simple table games requiring turns and observing rules, "school", feels pride clothes and accomplishments, eager to carry out some responsibility. **Intellectual Development** 2,072 words, tells long tales, carries out direction well, reads own name, counts to 10, asks meaning of words, knows colors, beginning to know difference between fact and fiction-lying, interested in environment, city, stores, etc

Chapter 4

MOTOR DEVELOPMENT

Motor development pervades all areas of development in the growing child. Motor skills enhance social behavior and they can benefit and support the development of cognition. We need to provide an environment for growth and development but in order to do this we must be knowledgeable about these areas. The infant can move from having little control over his or her body at birth, to sitting, standing and even walking in about a year.

There are individual behavioral differences for all children. For this reason, there are no norms for behavior listed, only a general age guideline for the development. We must keep in mind that each child is unique and he/she will develop at their own appropriate time. Motor development focuses on patterns of behavior rather than the attainment of such skills. These patterns of behavior can be seen as normal, delayed or what we call typical. Normal only refers to what the majority of children attain for their age.

The two main motor development principles are also used in the Aquatastic program. These two principles are prone and supine, which in layman's terms means front and back. The prone position in on the stomach while the supine position is on the back. Early motor development involves gaining control of the large or gross muscles in the body and then developing the smaller or fine muscles. When they accomplish this goal, the senses can be used to achieve aspects of motor development.

Gross motor development is the development and the coordination of the large muscles in the body. These muscles include the arms, legs, trunk and the neck. These muscles are used for sitting, standing and walking. The skills are also necessary to stabilize the body as the finer skills are performed. An infant's motor development is dependent on the very complex coordination of muscle tone and muscle strength. As with all developmental skills, practice opportunities are needed.

Once gross motor skills are attained the child can now master the fine motor skills. This area of development involves the coordination of the small muscles. The major accomplishment during this time period is that of reaching, grasping, and manipulation of objects. Motor development in the first few years of a child's life is phenomenal and will never again be seen like this in a person's lifetime. Growth, however, is not even and in some parts of the body will grow at different rates. There are variations in the rates of development but the patterns of development are relatively predictable at any given time period. By knowing the patterns of growth and understanding how they work we can properly assess the development of children. We need to plan their environments to stimulate and match their emerging skills.

Through the utilization of this knowledge we know what a comprehensive aquatic program should contain. We must prepare the beginner for a wide range of water safety, swimming and survival skills. We must provide opportunities for the child to apply the skills learned in the water to where drownings commonly occur, such as cold water. Lastly we must also include awareness and assessment segments designed to assist the individual to make appropriate judgments when they may be confronted with an emergency. We must make sure that we teach in an Aquatastic environment that is familiar and comfortable for the learner and it must also be easily accessible.

Motor development and swimming have a few objectives that are related to physical education. Organic development is achieved through fitness parameters such as cardio respiratory endurance, muscular endurance, flexibility, strength and power, which can all be achieved through Aquatastics. Muscular development is the coordination and agility that can be achieved through swimming, survival and rescue activities. Cognitive development is the recognition, assessment and decision making potential of the swimmer. This is how we measure the intellectual development of the individual. Personal and social development is seen through the interaction with other learners and through the cultivation of positive attitudes toward those in needs. We can see this as learning through experience. We need to keep trying and not to give up. Swimming takes time, patience and more patience. Perfect practice makes perfect swimming. Children need to be supervised at all times and it our job to make sure they are safe and develop to their fullest potential.

For too many years we have only had a vague notice of why the balanced motor development and movement education are important. The use of games, rhythms and self testing activities as well as concepts of space and relationship is viewed as a means to achieving increased skill rather than as an end in itself. Learning to move is too important to be left to chance or to the whims of untrained individuals. The individual with the knowledge can serve as a vital role in developing children's movement abilities as well as his or her physical abilities.

AQUATASTIC: SWIMMING MADE SIMPLE   *Ronda Brodsky*

Chapter 5

THE IMPORTANCE OF PLAY

Toys and equipment are often a valuable source of distraction as they help the fearful child feel more comfortable while gaining confidence. This will also give them a sense of familiarity and security as it is something they know and have seen before. As children become more comfortable and familiar the child will begin new methods of exploration in the Aquatastic environment.

Play is at the core of all developmentally appropriate activities. Play is a self motivated, freely chosen, process oriented and enjoyable activity. It allows the child an opportunity to create, invent, discover, and learn more about their world. It can also provide children with the joy and understanding of themselves and the people around them. Similar to child development, all children will go through stages of play. Each new experience opens up a wide world of opportunities around them.

Play to children is serious business, and it is this seriousness of purpose that supports play as an educational asset for development in children. Play is how children explore and experiment with the world around him or her. Play also allows children to build relations with others, the world and themselves. Children at play are discovering how to master new skills and how to gain confidence in themselves. Play serves as a medium through which children can learn through trial and error. They can experience a tremendous number of real life situations with minimal risks. It teaches children how to deal with the real world around him or her.

Play also helps develop the child mentally and emotionally. Some children may need to be taught how to play in a meaningful and constructive manner. Some children will exhibit their lack of ability to play through their wandering, constant boredom and even destructive play. When children play actively they will learn how to move for the sake of movement as well as learning how to play.

Play can allow a child to:

- use large and small muscles
- express and share feelings
- increase and stimulate their intellectual being

- develop and/or concentrate on attention span
- develop and increase use of their senses
- talk about their ideas and learn other ideas
- utilize the imagination and ability to be creative
- develop a positive self esteem and self concept
- have time to themselves to explore
- interact with others using many types of behavior

THERE are numerous areas of play development in which a child can and will go through. Unoccupied play will usually occur during the early stages of life. The child may not even look as though he or she is playing but they will be occupying themselves through their senses. Onlooker play is where they watch others and they are aware of what is going on around them. This behavior usually occurs in the toddlers. Solitary play also occurs with the toddler and this is when the child is playing alone but he or she is within earshot of his parent or caregiver. Parallel play can be seen in the older toddler and young preschooler. They are usually next to another child and both of them are playing with the same toy but in different ways. They may not even be aware of the other child. Associative play is when the three and four year olds begin to play in groups. They generally use the same toys but they may be doing their own thing. Cooperative play is usually organized and can be seen by the older preschooler. Dramatic play is seen in young children through the use of objects and toys. This type of play allows the child to imitate what he or she has seen other adults do. A recognizable form of dramatic play would be the use of superheroes in the child's play.

As teachers we have the responsibility to make sure children are playing. Play can be a very valuable asset in assessing a child's stage of development. We can help them attain a positive self esteem and self concept through the use of play. As instructors we need to respect and encourage individual differences in all abilities of play. We definitely need patience and we need to allow children the freedom to play as they wish. Encouraging cooperation will help the child get to the next stage of development and it will also teach them common courtesy. Lastly we need to take time to listen to children and observe how they play. Play is vital and we need to help children develop to their fullest potential. Play, toys and play spaces are important to children of all ages. We need to let our children play and gain these skills to develop to a well rounded individual.

In play, a child is totally involved, he or she moves, thinks and feels. Through play a child learns to control him or herself and objects in the environment as he or she works against gravity, and to move in and through spaces. Play will become socialized as the child seeks out others for cooperative or competitive games and activities. Whether we call it physical education or play, it all serves the same purpose. The objective here is to meet the needs of each child.

Effective instructors or play leaders should model and value fair play. These people should try to tone down any rivalries, avoid rejection or any elimination games. Accomplishments should be praised in addition to good sportsmanlike behavior. These leaders should also demonstrate enthusiasm, cooperation and teamwork among the joy of playing. We have to do as we say and lead by example in all we do.

Play has many purposes: muscular development, motor and physical development; social interaction; and self realization. It can truly be said that play or physical education has an important contribution and impact to make in the developmental process through which children come to know themselves. Children best learn through play. Play is the goal for all children during childhood. Children learn through play and fun, but they will need lots of positive guidance and encouragement through the way. Play leaders or physical educators will and can guide the use of play rather than utilizing the standard educational methods or that of formal lectures to the child. All teachers can be play leaders and they all need to focus on the FUNdamentals of childhood learning – PLAY.

AQUATIC GAMES:

Webster defines aquatics as taking place in or about the water and games as an activity engaged in for diversion or amusement. Looking at these definitions aquatic games can be defined as activities engaged in for amusement in or around the water. As stated previously, the goal of child development as well as the goal of physical education is through the physical, mental and social development of each person. Our goal here is achieved through the use of aquatic games.

AQUATASTIC: SWIMMING MADE SIMPLE *Ronda Brodsky*

There are many possible learning objectives that can be attained through the use of aquatic games. The development of useful and fun aquatic skills through the use of physical activity is just one of these objectives. You can develop and maintain major physical efficiency through activities in and around the aquatic environment. Sportsmanship or acting in a socially acceptable way may also be achieved. Lastly aquatic games can be used for recreational purposes.

There are a few things that must be taken into consideration before using aquatic games. Safety is a number one priority in and around the pool area and environment. You should know how to prevent and deal with any accidents that may occur. You need to maintain and keep track of the aquatic environment that you will be utilizing. Appropriate games for students must be used as you should not use a deep water game for beginner swimmers. You need to match the skills of the students to the skill or skills of the game being played. The aquatic environment must constantly and effectively be scanned and supervised. All safety rules and regulations must be adhered to in the aquatic environment. Once these safety measures have been secured and achieved it is now time to have fun in your Aquatastic swimming environment.

One game that my team's swimmers love to play is sharks and minnow. This can work anywhere as long as you can keep swimmers safe and have two separate target areas, called safe zones in this game:

- A few swimmers are selected to be sharks, and they get to roam around the central part of the pool.
- The rest of the swimmers line up in a safe zone on one side of the swimming pool (the minnows).
- We leave all lane lines in the pool and the last line on each side of the swimming pool are the safe zones. Depending upon the skill level of the group playing, we expand or contract the size of the safe zone and the size of the area that is "legally" useable for crossing between safe zones.
- On a signal, the minnows must swim to the opposite side of the pool to reach the other safe zone.
- If a shark touches any part of a minnow while any part of a minnow is above water, the minnow is caught and becomes a shark.
- When only a few minnows are left, the sharks and minnows switch and we play again.

Penny Hunt

Throw a large amount of pennies (depending on the number of kids) into a good size pool. Cover about a third of the pennies with white out and send the children in to dive for them. If a child find a penny with white out, that child gets a prize. Great for all ages! Shallow for the youngest and deeper for the older kids.

Cannonball Contest

Have two groups; one for the cannonballs and the other group a team of judges. The cannonball group line up behind a diving board and have to make the biggest splash to get the higest vote. The judges are the voters and give each person a vote out of ten. An adult is needed to decide what the majority of the judges want to give each person.

Frozen Tag

Preferably in a smaller pool; it's just like regular frozen tag, but once tagged, a person has to swim under your legs to free you.

MARCO POLO

In Marco Polo you need at least 3 people. one of them is IT. Whoever is chosen to be IT has to close his/her eyes (cover with hands) and then count out loud numbers from 1 to 10. After IT has counted to 10, then IT begins to search for the other players with his or hers remaining closed. If the person that is IT wants to he/she can call out "Marco" the other players then must say "Polo" The Person who is IT searches for people and if IT tags someone then he/she becomes the new IT.

Races / Competitions

Remember to keep the courses safe and use your own common sense, such as use of the shallow end for swimmers who are not confident in the water. Possible races can include

- Obstacle courses... include things such as swimming through hoops, pushing a ball through the water. Swimming underwater, retrieving objects from the bottom of the pool, etc. But
- Distance under water,
- Time under water

Chapter 6

An infant is any child under the age of one. Infants have a lot to learn from the aquatic environment, but the key for infants is comfort. They need to feel safe in their environment. Infants need to learn to be in harmony with the water and the aquatic environment. As instructors we need to teach infants and children to respect the water and we need to respect our students throughout the learning process.

Infants will learn how to take turns, to follow directions and socializing with someone other than their parents. They will learn how to separate from their parents and to trust other adults as he or she develops motor skills. The child will also learn communication skills while learn to be more independent in the water. In addition to all of this, the child will also gain water safety habits. Young children gain confidence, exercise and coordination but they must be watched carefully and encouraged constantly as they are in the aquatic environment. Remember the key here, as it is in the Aquatastic environment is to have fun and always smile as you learn.

When teaching children of all ages you must consider each child's rate of learning. This rate will vary from person to person and you should encourage each child at his or her own rate of learning. You need to find their comfort level and teach there while remembering that learning is sequential and water familiarization develops over time. You will need to focus on buoyancy, mobility and body orientation for each child. From there you may move on to propulsion, stroke exploration and stroke development.

Water familiarization will help to develop familiarity, freedom of movement and enjoyment in the water. Children will acquire the confidence necessary to progress to other stages of learning. Buoyancy, mobility and body orientation will increase the learners to control and understand how he or she floats in the water. Mobility skills will be developed which will help the learner to propel him or herself confidently through the water. He or she will also begin to understand the mechanics of propulsion and help the learners orientate their bodies from a variety of positions to a safe recovery position while developing rotation skills.

For propulsion and stroke exploration to occur the child should have undergone a wide range of experiences that should have led to confidence, buoyancy and mobility in the water. This stage should help them learn the basic techniques of stroke development. Stroke exploration enables learners to experience the necessary coordination in each stroke. Sculling is the basic movement or propulsive stroke here and you need to remember that bad habits should be corrected and not be allowed to continue at this point.

Stroke development should occur from the simple to the more complex. The front and back crawl generally are taught as the first real swimming strokes. The breast stroke and the elementary backstroke generally come next. Being able to mix the elements of various strokes is a valuable skill and should be encouraged as the basic strokes become mastered.

Here are some helpful hints for a great experience:
- Group praise gives encouragement and reinforcement needs to be positive as fun and excitement are needed
- Be flexible and let your body be your guide – work with your child not against them – ease into the tasks and show encouragement with each new task
- Be gentle – use slow movements and always be ready to cuddle the child
- Be careful and keep an eye on the child to make sure he or she is not drinking too much water –a drink of juice before class may decrease the chances of drinking pool water
- Develop an atmosphere of you and the child and concentrate on what you are doing
- Do not ask if the child wants to do something – use a calm, friendly voice to inform him or her of the next activity – do not hesitate as that causes confusion and makes the child unsure of what to do
- You need to establish trust and follow through on tasks
- Younger children are usually more relaxed and respond more readily to holding their breath – they may still have a kicking reflex and they may be more relaxed
- Horizontal submersions are not advised as it is better for the child to naturally go under the water by him or herself or to put the face in on their own
- The Aquatastic way is to never force a child to do anything they are not comfortable doing – especially forcing a child to go under water when he or she is not ready

Infant Aquatics: (birth – 15 months)

Infants can learn a lot in the aquatic environment. They can learn about harmony in the water and respect for the water and the aquatic environment. The key here is comfort for the infant and the person in the water with the infant. There are many benefits for infant aquatics. Amongst these benefits are socialization, taking turns, following directions, separation from parents, developing motor and communication skills and water safety habits.

Infant aquatics should teach safe movements and be about learning together in water while you play and have fun. It is about helping your child feel comfortable in the water safely as we build up confidence in water through encouragement, exploration and in support. Prepare before going to the water with your child by taking and using the right equipment. You'll also need to check the environment and plan an emergency response in case there is a problem. You need to stay safe by properly supporting and supervising your child. In order to survive you need to know how to perform a rescue and get help for your child.

In water you should be aware of your child development is most infants through the age 15 months will enjoy sounds, , rhythms, songs, bright colors and objects. The child will move instinctively in the water with little control or coordination. The child can hold objects, mimics simple actions and sounds. You'll need support and constant supervision as you care for your child. Use a calm positive and reassuring voice and make sure your child will recognize you in the water. If you wear glasses wear them in the water. Prepare your child for each movement or activity. The gentle and slow, use clues such as 1-2-3 or Ready – Set - Go.

Swimming lessons are very different than a bath. You need to date used to supporting and moving in a child through the water. Getting wet helps the child experience the feel water has on the body. Buoyancy and movement can be used by rocking and turning the child in the water. Exhaling through the mouth can be done by blowing bubbles at the surface of the water. A basic kick and basic arm action move the child's arms and legs while encouraging independent movement. Submersion at this age can be done if you want to gently go under the water if the child is comfortable and ready.

Toddler Aquatics (16-24 months)

Help your child become comfortable water and explore different types of safe water movement. Children will progress at their own pace and most children at this age will enjoy games. Additionally they will enjoy activities, rhythms and song, as well as independent play. Basic coordination can help the child understand and relate to simple instructions. You'll need patience, variety, as well as constant supervision and support. Help your child explore the water through the use of flotation and movement. The best skills to work on are: getting wet; buoyancy and movement; exhaling through the mouth; floats; glides; and the front swam.

Children should be taught based on their readiness to learn as there is no specific age at which a child should be taught to swim, however, if they are in a formal education setting it will be easier for them to learn. While the child is having a bath it should be a pleasant experience and the emphasis should be placed on fun and laughter. These bath times are important and vital for developing a child's water confidence and comfort level. If the child has a fear of the water it can be best dealt with water confidence and trust in the instructor.

Preschool aquatics (24 to 36 months)

At this stage you need to encourage children to move, float and swim safely as well as being independent. These children progress at their own rate or pace and they need encouragement and support in the water. Most children at this stage enjoy showing, watching, exploring, experimenting movements with more control and coordination. The dog paddling motions and frog motions in the water can help the child understand what is right and what is wrong in the water. You need to encourage a child to move, as well as float and swim a independently. The main skill noted at this age are: getting wet; rhythmic breathing; front and back floats and glides; front and back kicks; front and back glides with a flutter kick; changing direct; and the front swim.

The preschool child is different than the elementary or even the Kindergarten child. These young children will have different physical, social and emotional needs. Their cognitive needs will also vary in abilities. Elementary class structure should not be used with the preschool child. It is recommended that the preschool class is no longer than thirty minutes in length. Children at this age, and at many ages, are best taught new skills when the activities are changed frequently as to prevent boredom or loss of attention. Generally in a thirty minute class the child will be introduced or working on 4-5 different skills. Each one of these activities will be around 5-6 minutes in length a piece. These activities would then be re-introduced and used throughout the course of the lessons.

Whatever structure you choose, remember that in order to be successful you will need to provide more than one developmentally appropriate activity per lesson taught. Once you have accomplished this you must remember to re-teach these skills in order to perfect them.

AQUATASTIC GENERAL TEACHING STRATEGIES

Introduce yourself at the beginning of each class. Make sure that your students know your name. Get to know your students by name and face. Use as many games as possible as children need to have fun while learning. If children are having fun they will learn but they may not realize that they are learning. Focus on fun as they do not need to know that they are learning. Remember that swimming the Aquatastic way is FUNdamental.

GETTING FACE WET:
- Ring toss to the bottom
- Diving discs or toys on the bottom or on the steps depending on the age and ability
- Ring around the Rosie
- If you are Happy and you know it …
- Look for fish in the pool
- Wash face with a sponge or other water toy
- Start getting the face wet body part by body part, i.e. Ears, nose, chin, cheeks, forehead, back of head etc.

WATER ACCLIMATION:
- Sponges – wash body parts
- Bowls of water to pour on body parts
- Make rain drops using hands, sieves, flower pots, water wheels or sprinklers

BUBBLE BLOWING:
- Pretend to blow candles on a birthday cake
- Practice blowing on a straw or pretend the water is a straw
- Talk like a fish underwater
- Use a pinwheel and then put it in the water
- Blow ping pong balls across the pool
- Blow as if the water is hot

KICKING:
- Pretend to be a motor boat
- Kick splashing the water keeping your feet at the surface
- Make the water bubble and boil as you are kicking
- Practice kicking on the steps while sitting on your bottom
- Practice kicking on the steps while putting your hands on the steps as you

are on your stomach
- Practice kicking on the barbell with your arms over the barbell
- Once comfortable with that move on to holding the barbell with you hands and kicking
- Once confident and comfortable work your way to a kickboard
- Once confident and comfortable work your way to kicking on you own with no flotation devices

ARM MOTION:
- Reach and pull as if you are trying to grab something in front of you
- Stretch and reach forward
- Once you can do this motion you begin with the arms out of the water as in the freestyle
- Once confident add the arms and legs together

FLOATING:
<u>Back</u>:
- look for birds – look in the sky
- Just like you are sleeping on your back
- Airplane arms
- On your knees lean back to float
- Back float with assistance as you lean on the instructor's shoulder
- Back float on your own
- Kick and move your arms on your back
- Start back and float from the wall

<u>Front</u>:
- just like sleeping on your stomach
- Prone glide on stomach to instructor with assistance
- Prone glide on stomach to instructor without assistance
- Once confident and comfortable add kicking
- Once confident and comfortable add arms to the kicking

TEACHING 3-5 YEAR OLDS THE AQUATASTIC WAY

1. Do not strive for absolute perfection. Perfection comes with time.
2. Do not let children in before the start of their lesson as they may tire out too quickly.
3. Children should have nothing in their mouths.
4. It normally takes at least 10 lessons to teach a 3 year old to float face down.
5. Be patient and kind.
6. Do not use big words. Use words that the children can understand and follow.
7. Use common words like: go under – come up – blow out – take a big

breath.
8. First lesson, you should tell the child your name and you should get to know all the students names.
9. Take children's hands and start walking in the shallow part of the pool until they are more comfortable and confident in their aquatic abilities.
10. Be truthful at all times. If you trick them to do something they will have lost all of their trust in you. No surprises to these children and you need to make sure you tell them what is coming next.

INSTRUCTION: ASK KEY QUESTIONS.

1. Teacher should be in the water waist high. Have all children sit on the edge and kick. Repeat a couple of times. Make sure you are on the child's level.
2. Use a barbell or swim bar. Place the child's arms over it and hold his or her hands if they need additional support.
3. Make sure their arms are fully extended and paddling like a dog. Their feet should be kicking, preferably splashing the water.
4. As you walk backwards, continue talking to the child while reinforcing the skills to be done, and getting his or her mind off being hesitant in the water or on the barbell.
5. Slowly work your hands away from the child's hand so he or she can do the dog paddle on the barbell by themselves.
6. In the first couple of lessons, follow the child's instincts so the child has time to adjust to you. After this the child WILL begin to trust you.
7. After the first lesson the child should feel more comfortable in the water.
8. Never take your eyes off the child or children for any reason. Children can drown in 2-3 seconds in as little as 1 inch of water. Constant vigilance is the key to safety.

BLOWING BUBBLES FOR THE REAL BEGINNERS:

1. Ask them to show you how to blow a bubble if they can.
2. Tell them to blow as if they were using a straw. Pinwheels are great for getting the beginner to blow a bubble. Store bought bubbles also work well but I would not advise them as they make the pool surface and deck very slippery. Remind them to blow the water as if they are blowing out birthday cake candles.
3. When they are ready they may begin to do underwater bubbles. When you want them to put their face in the water and to hold their breath, say: on the count of 3 I want you to hold your breath and put your face in. If you need to you may get them comfortable with putting their faces in body part by body part such as the chin or the forehead.
4. When saying take a big breath, you should first demonstrate how you

want it done. Lead by example as children will best learn from a visual like watching you.
5. Once a child can hold his or her breath without trouble and without too much effort, the child is then ready to learn how to float. They may float before this but until they put their faces in they cannot achieve a real float.

LEARNING TO FLOAT:

1. If the water is shallow have children kneel down, arms outstretched, leaning forward putting their face in the water.
2. Next, stand in the shallow part of the pool; you should stand back while the child practices this. Hold your arms out ready to catch him or her and have them stretch their arms toward you. This can also be done by having the child hold the wall with both hands facing the wall elevating his or her legs out. Once this is accomplished you can have the child put 1 hand on the wall facing you and the other toward you. Have the child push off the wall like Superman and swim to you. You must remain within arms length of the child to begin with and as the child gets more comfortable you can back up.
3. Next is to get them kicking in the water. Have the child glide (a Superman) off the wall and add the kick. Once they are able to kick have the child kick with his or her face in the water.
4. Have the child take a deep breath, face in the water, move his or her arms and kick the feet while splashing in the water. Have the child practice the arms out of the water reaching for something in front of him or her.
5. Walk backwards from the child, encouraging him or her to do it by themselves. You must stay near the child so they know that you are near if they need help or assistance.
6. If the legs are trailing too low, lift them up by pushing their hips up. Remind the child to kick on top of the water by splashing the water. If the arms splash out too much, push the arms down and remind the child to bring the arm out of the water from the elbow to the fingertips.
7. Remember to praise the child as positive reinforcement and encouragement is very important to the child.

OPENING EYES UNDER WATER:

1. While the child is floating ask him or her to open their eyes under water and see if they can see your feet or legs.
2. Play the number game with them. Put one hand under water and have the child identify how many fingers you have up. This game is best done with children that know their numbers. With younger children you may want to use toys that are easy to pick up as to build upon their confidence level.

3. Another game is for you to go under water with the child but you must first make sure you tell the child what you are doing. This is not recommended for any child that is fearful in the water.
4. One more game to play would be to make faces at each other under water. Once you submerge have the child describe your expression.

KICKING AND FLOATING ON THE BACK:
1. To teach 3-5 year olds to float and kick on their backs, use the same as any child. The barbell is best used to give the child confidence to float on his or her back.
2. Always stand behind the child supporting their heads in one hand correcting the body position by touch until he or she floats.

WHAT YOU NEED TO GO SWIMMING: BASIC SWIMMING GEAR
- Swimsuit - wear something comfortable
- Goggles – to keep your eyes protected
- Bathing Cap – to keep your hair out of your eyes
- Kickboards
- Pull Buoys
- Fins or flippers
- Barbells or swim bars
- Towel – to dry off with after you are done
- Sunscreen – to stay safe in the sun
- Sunglasses – to protect your eyes

Remember to shower after you get out of the pool to rid your body of chlorine and other pool chemicals. Soap and water work but shampoo works better. I have personally found that the best way for keeping your hair looking good is by continuously switching shampoo and conditioners. My shower tends to have 3-4 different kinds in there at one time. Once you are done showering it is also best to use lotion on your skin to maintain its natural moisture.

Goggles let you see and focus where you are going and you can better see what you are doing underwater. They also help protect your eyes from chlorine and other pool chemicals as they may irritate your eyes after being in the water.

Kickboards help keep you buoyant (afloat) while you focus on one aspect of a swimming stroke. Kickboards will help you work on your lower body and kicking for the different swimming strokes.

Fins or flippers help keep the body horizontal and gives you more flexibility especially where you need it in the ankles. These can also help you work on your leg strokes and your leg muscles.

I only use barbells or swim bars for children as they learn to swim. I will never use water wings as I pop them as they give the child a false sense of security. Life jackets may be used but you must remember to have the child stay in the proper swimming position.

Sunscreen and sunglasses are vital to me and I see them as a necessity to properly teach a class. This will help protect you so you can continue teaching. Teaching children this at a young age will help to keep them swimming safely outdoors.

SWIMMING STROKES

Swimming is the act of moving through the water via the use of arms, legs and bodies. We call this movement swimming strokes. The most well known strokes in the crawl or the freestyle, the back crawl or the backstroke, the breast stroke, the side stroke and the butterfly.

Many people believe that humans are born with a swimming ability, an innate sense of swimming and staying afloat using one's arms and legs. People can swim in any body of water that will allow the individual room to move about. These bodies may include lakes, rivers, the ocean and pools. The average water temperature is between 68-84 degrees. The temperature will vary depending on the weather and the environment. Many indoor pools keep their temperature at 82 as this is the best environment to do most aquatic activities. When teaching younger children you may want to find an aquatic environment where the water is at least 84 as it will be more comfortable for them and they will not chill as quickly.

Humans have been swimming for thousands of years. One of the earliest noted experiences is believed to be Pharaoh Ramses II (1290-1224 BC) of Egypt. Swimming in Ancient Greece and Rome was highly esteemed and it was used as a form of training for the warriors. By around 1896 swimming had become well known and established. It was one of the main sports at the first modern Olympic Games held in Athens Greece. Swimming should always be fun so go jump in and have an Aquatastic time.

COMMON FEATURES OF SWIMMING STROKES

- **Pitch of the Hand:** use a curved pattern and the hands should be cupped and not flat
- **Curved pathway pull:** hands must continually from a straight line when contacting the still water – If the hand goes in a straight line little propulsion will be seen because the hand is going against the moving water. An S pattern will help ensure the hand works against the water to propel the individual through the water.
- **Hand entry and exit:** enter and exit the water cleanly. Enter at an angle to prevent dragging of the water. Hands should leave the water clearly as to avoid dangers of dragging or slowing the swimmer down.
- **Pushing and pulling:** the arms bend and straighten during these phases. The elbow is held high when swimming on the front and the elbow is held low when swimming on the back.
- **Streamlining:** keep your body horizontal to the surface of the water to reduce resistance. Pull the water from the front and push it back. This horizontal position must be maintained at all times. To create as little resistance as possible, the individual should try to keep the body movement to a minimum when possible.

FREESTYLE OR FRONT CRAWL

The freestyle or front crawl is the fastest and most efficient swimming strokes, and this is usually what makes it pretty popular. This stroke can get very tiring as the arms are generally out of the water. There are many variations and tricks to better swimming this stroke but these are the keys that I teach in the Aquatastic method.

Body Position
- the body is on the front – flat, streamlined and as horizontal as possible
- the waterline should be at the top of the forehead
- the angle of the body can be adjusted by the position of the head as raising the head will lower the feet

- Leg Movement
  - the legs should be able to hold the body in a stable and streamlined position at all times
  - the legs help move and propel the body through the water
  - the movement should come from the hips in a rhythmical up and down motion, and it should be done continuously
  - the legs should be relaxed with the knees bent a bit
  - the ankles should be kept flexible and loose at all times
  - the feet should just touch and skim the surface of the water

Arm Movement
- alternate the movement of the arms with one always under water as the other arm is recovering
- enter the water in front of that shoulder with the thumb first at a 45 degree angle as to avoid too much resistance
- move the hands backward in a S pattern bending the elbow half way through the stroke
- the elbow should be higher than the hand at all times and be pointed sideways
- half way through this motion the elbow should be straightened by pushing the hand backward and out through the hips
- throughout the stroke the hand should pitch in across the body and out as the arm will extend
- the arm should recover in a relaxed way via the use of momentum
- the elbow should be carried high with the hand close to the body and near the surface of the water, which is the recovery stage of the stroke
- keep the recovery close to the body as too wide of a recovery can lead to swinging of the hips and should not be done

Breathing
- arm action causes the body to naturally roll
- to breathe the head should roll with the body and not lifted out of the water
- should be started while pushing the arm out of the water
- should be done through the mouth or through the mouth and nose
- should not turn the face all of the way out of the water as you only need a portion out big enough for you to breathe
- should start immediately after the mouth leaves the surface of the water
- should continue non stop until the mouth is back in the water
- can be done on either side, choose the more comfortable side or if wanted you may breathe bilaterally or on both sides
- focus on breathing right as perfect practice makes perfect

The arm recovery usually takes less time than the underwater stroke so that one arm should enter as the other is about halfway through the underwater stroke. The timing of the leg action should be allowed to occur naturally. The leg action will be dependent upon the arm action.

BACK CRAWL – BACKSTROKE

The back crawl is the only competitive stroke swum on the back and breathing is relatively easy as your face is generally out of the water. As you swim on your back it is difficult to see where you are going so you must properly learn how to judge this and learn how to see where you are going.

Body Position
- the body should be stretched out on the back in a streamlined position with the hips relatively close to the surface of the water
- you can best adjust your body position by tilting the head
- the head should be steady as the body rolls naturally as the arms recover
- do not tuck your chin too tightly to the chest as it may cause the hips to drop and ruin the streamlining

Leg Movement
- the legs will help maintain a streamlined body position
- should be a continuous wave motion of alternating feet
- the toes should barely be seen over the surface of the water
- flexibility should be continual in the ankles and legs
- ankles and feet should be relaxed with the toes not pointed

Arm Movement
- as the arm enters the water the little finger should be first as it should be directly behind that shoulder
- as the hand makes contact with the water, you begin the back stroke
- the natural roll of the body toward the arm entering the water will help the hand reach the correct depth to begin pulling
- at the beginning of the pull, the elbow should begin to bend
- the elbow bend should increase to a 90 degree angle as the hand passes the shoulder when the push begins
- the elbow straightens during the push as the hand pushes back and down in a curved path
- the hand should finish with the palm facing down – this will help the body roll away from that arm as the other arm enters the water
- the recovery over the water is relaxed but straight with the palm facing out sideways as the little finger enters the water first

BREAST STROKE

The breast stroke is an easy and relaxing stroke, but as a competitive stroke it uses more energy than any other stroke. As in the other strokes you need to maintain a streamlined body position. This stroke is continuously going through changes and this is generally how I teach this stroke.

Body Position
- should be kept as flat as possible in the water to reduce the amount of resistance
- the head will be raised later in the stroke to minimize the shoulders from coming out of the water due to the arm stroke
- the legs will recover by bending the knees and hips so to keep the hips high in the water
- heels are close to the surface but the feet do not break the surface of the water

Leg Movement
- can provide tremendous power
- recover from an extended position as they bend through the knees and hips
- feet start together but may separate to about shoulder width as the knees fully flex
- toes should be moving toward the shin
- before starting the kick the feet should be facing outward and the ankles should be flexed
- kick starts by thrusting feet apart and backwards with the heels tracing a circular pattern as they move backwards
- at the end the feet come together after the legs straighten out
- you should feel the water pressure on the soles and the inside of the feet

Arm Movement
- press arms down and out in a diagonal motion with the hands
- at the maximum width of the pull, the elbows should bend as the hands propel toward the center of the body
- a high elbow position should be seen and maintained until the hands finish the movement in
- the hands will glide forward as the arms fully extend

Breathing
- breathing should be done on every stroke
- lift the head out as you extend the neck at the end of the pulling of the arms and breathe in
- return the face to the water right before the arms fully extend while breathing out
- the water level will generally stay between the chin while breathing in and the forehead as you breathe out

When learning to swim this stroke, a glide should be used after the kick and before the next arm stroke starts. The body should be at a full stretch during the glide. Make sure to fully extend the glide before beginning the next stroke. The arms and legs should work in sequence to produce a fluid style with your stroke. When the arms work the legs will recover and when the legs work the arms will recover. The arms and legs are constantly working together to propel the body through the water. There should be little activity above the water in this stroke as most of the stroke should be at water level.

SIDE STROKE

The side stroke evolved from the breast stroke as people thought it would be easier as you remained on your side the whole time. As it turns out it is slower as the stroke generates less force than other strokes. The side stroke is now mainly used for recreation and survival water rescue. You should be able to swim the side stroke on both sides and it does not matter which side is used as it is a personal preference.

Body Position
- stretch the body out on the side in a relaxed and streamlined position as horizontal as possible
- one side of the head is always in the water

Leg Movement
- the leg stroke is generally called the scissors kick
- bend – open – kick – glide are the 4 phases of the kick
- recovering is done by placing the legs in a relaxed manner with the hips and knees slightly bending as the legs and feet are placed together
- the shins should be in line with the middle of the body
- the legs are opened by moving the top leg forward and the bottom leg backward
- ankle of the top leg should have the toes drawn up toward the shins and the ankle of the bottom leg with the toes pointed
- the legs are opened wide, kicked back as the feet are brought together
- water pressure may be felt on the sole of the foot and on the back of the foot
- the legs are then held together with the toes pointed as the body propels with a short glide through the water

Arm Movement
- while gliding the bottom arm should be extended fully beyond the head just below the surface of the water
- the top arm should be extended along the body with the hand just below the surface of the water
- pull back in a curved pathway as the elbow bend progressively until the hand is even with the shoulders
- the hand should then pass near the chin as the hand is pushed forward to

- a glide position
- the top arm then recovers close to the thigh as the hand strongly pushes through the water
- the arm should remain extended for the duration of the glide
- I generally teach this as I tell the student to glide the hand upward to pick an apple off the tree and then to gently slide it along the body to put the apple in the basket by the hip

Breathing

- should take place through the mouth during the pull of the bottom arm
- if needed you may turn your head to get more air
- it is relatively easy to breathe in this stroke as half of your face is usually out of the water

BUTTERFLY

This is a more advanced stroke and can be very difficult to do as you will need good technique is this powerful and graceful stroke. This is a great stroke for developing flexibility, strength and definitely endurance. It can be very strenuous as it uses both arms out of the water at a time.

Body Position

- the body is stretched on the front and it is as flat as possible while remaining in a streamlined position
- the hips should be kept close to the surface
- if the head is held too high or if a poor kick is used the hips may drop will increase the resistance

Leg Movement

- the leg action is up and down as if you were a dolphin
- the ankles and knees should be relaxed
- the legs are straight in an upward motion
- the heels barely break the surface of the water at the top of the kick
- knees should bend to do a whip like movement on the downward motion

Arm Movement

- the hands should pretend they are an hourglass as they as perform the arm movement
- the hands sweep out and around to a position together under the chest
- elbows are kept high to prevent hands from getting out of position
- the hands push back and out as the elbows begin to straighten
- pushing hard at the end of the movement will help with the beginning of the recovery
- while the arms are relaxed the recovery is made over the water

Breathing
- as the hands enter the water breathing should begin slowly finishing with a forceful breath of air before the mouth clears the water to breathe in
- breathing in should begin at the last stage of the push and be completed by the middle of the recovery stroke
- the face returns to the water before the hands re-enter the water

Timing
- the legs should kick twice per each arm movement
- hands enters the water and the arms push forward
- the timing will begin to occur naturally as it will help propel the body forward through the water as the body is streamlined
- the hips are close to the surface which will in turn make it easier to lift the head to get a breath

SWIMMING UNDER THE WATER
- best achieved when done with the breaststroke arm movement and the breaststroke kick
- can be used to propel through the water
- can be used to locate something in the water that may be under the water
- can be used to escape danger on the surface of the water
- if fins are available they will help propel you through the water at greater speeds while using the front crawl kick
- water pressure increases as you go further in the water
- depths deeper than 3 meters may cause ear pain unless the pressure is equalized (holding the nose while blowing out or exhaling water through the nose)
- you can also attempt to equalize the pressure by swallowing or moving the jaw

ENTRIES AND EXITS INTO THE WATER IN THE AQUATASTIC ENVIRONMENT:

There are numerous ways to get in the pool. It all depends on the aquatic environment, the age of the child and the ability of the child. You need to do what you are comfortable with but you first must make sure it is safe for you and everyone around you.

- The slide in entry – this is best used when the depth of the water and the status of the bottom is unknown. This entry is controlled and safe and it allows for the feet to feel for the unknown obstacles below the surface. You first need to establish a firm body position either by sitting or lying the lower body gently. Take the weight onto the hands and face the side as it permits greater control for raising and lowering the body.
- The step in entry – this is best used when the water is clear, the depth is known and the bottom is free of obstacles. This is also known as a jump in entry. Look at the point of entry and step (not jump) gently from the edge keeping the knees slightly flexed and the legs ready to give when the feet touch the bottom. Always go in feet first to lessen the chance of injury and do not panic. This is mainly used as a confidence building activity. Once you gain confidence you may do this in the deep end of the pool.
- Sitting on the side entry – Sit on the shallow end of the pool facing the water. Slowly twist your body as your hands are on the side and gently ease yourself in backwards. You can also use this method as an exit, but

this time you put your hands on the side and twist yourself as you gently position your body to sitting on the edge of the pool.
- Steps or ladder – in the pool. With the steps hold on to the pole or railing and gently walk into the water. Always use the steps if you are at all hesitant about the aquatic environment. You climb out the steps the opposite way you climbed in always facing the pole and holding on to it. With the ladder, hold the rail and go down backwards, slowly step by step holding on to the railings. When you reach the bottom you may let go and if you need to you may hold on to the side wall. Hopefully you are in water that is not too deep or over your head. Hold on to the rail at all times and try not to tense your feet as you ease yourself into the pool. Choose a comfortable part of the pool, one where you can feel confident about your aquatic skills and/or one where you can comfortably stand on the bottom of the pool. To exit the pool from the ladder just face the ladder and gently step your way up to the top making sure you continue to face the ladder.

- Diving – this can only be done with supervision in deep water, preferably over 9 feet of water. You must always do a shallow dive to prevent injuries by hitting the bottom of the pool. The dive is generally done standing up but it is taught in progression from easiest to hardest. The first step is sitting on the edge or on the diving board. The second step is kneeling with one knee down and the foot other foot forward on the edge of the pool or on the diving board. The last step is done by standing upright on the edge of the pool or on the diving board. Each step is done in a similar manner as you sit over the edge of the pool with the feet facing down. Your hands are over your head with the elbows against the ears. The goal of any dive is to land hands first into the pool. The feet should be the last body part to enter the water.

Chapter 7

GENERAL WATER SAFETY TIPS

- Learn to swim. The best thing anyone can do to stay safe in and around the water is to learn to swim. Always swim with a buddy; never swim alone. The American Red Cross has swimming courses for people of any age and swimming ability. To enroll in a swim course, contact your local Red Cross chapter.
- Select a supervised area. A trained lifeguard who can help in an emergency is the best safety factor. Even good swimmers can have an unexpected medical emergency in the water. Never swim alone.
- Obey all rules and posted signs.
- Watch out for the "dangerous too's"--too tired, too cold, too far from safety, too much sun, too much strenuous activity.
- Don't mix alcohol and swimming. Alcohol impairs your judgment, balance, and coordination, affects your swimming and diving skills, and reduces your body's ability to stay warm.
- Pay attention to local weather conditions and forecasts. Stop swimming at the first indication of bad weather.
- Know how to prevent, recognize, and respond to emergencies.

Beach Safety
- Protect your skin: Sunlight contains two kinds of UV rays -- UVA increases the risk of skin cancer, skin aging, and other skin diseases. UVB causes sunburn and can lead to skin cancer. Limit the amount of direct sunlight you receive between 10:00 a.m. and 4:00 p.m. and wear a sunscreen with a sun protection factor containing a high rating such as 15.
- Drink plenty of water regularly and often even if you do not feel thirsty. Your body needs water to keep cool. Avoid drinks with alcohol or caffeine in them. They can make you feel good briefly but make the heat's effects on your body worse. This is especially true with beer, which dehydrates the body.
- Watch for signs of heat stroke: Heat stroke is life-threatening. The victim's temperature control system, which produces sweating to cool the body,

stops working. The body temperature can rise so high that brain damage and death may result if the body is not cooled quickly. Signals include hot, red, and dry skin; changes in consciousness, rapid, weak pulse, and rapid, shallow breathing. Call 9-1-1 or your local EMS number. Move the person to a cooler place. Quickly cool the body by wrapping wet sheets around the body and fan it. If you have ice packs or cold packs, place them on each of the victim's wrists and ankles, in the armpits and on the neck to cool the large blood vessels. Watch for signals of breathing problems and make sure the airway is clear. Keep the person lying down.
- Wear eye protection: Sunglasses are like sunscreen for your eyes and protect against damage that can occur from UV rays. Be sure to wear sunglasses with labels that indicate that they absorb at least 90 percent of UV sunlight.
- Wear foot protection: Many times, people's feet can get burned from the sand or cut from glass in the sand.

Boating
- Learn to swim. The best thing anyone can do to stay safe in and around the water is to learn to swim. This includes anyone participating in any boating activity. The American Red Cross has swimming courses for people of any age and swimming ability. To enroll in a swim course, contact your local Red Cross chapter.
- Alcohol and boating don't mix. Alcohol impairs your judgment, balance, and coordination -- over 50 percent of drownings result from boating incidents involving alcohol. For the same reasons it is dangerous to operate an automobile while under the influence of alcohol, people should not operate a boat while drinking alcohol.
- Look for the label: Use Coast Guard-approved life jackets for yourself and your passengers when boating and fishing.
- Develop a float plan. Anytime you go out in a boat, give a responsible person details about where you will be and how long you will be gone. This is important because if the boat is delayed because of an emergency, becomes lost, or encounters other problems, you want help to be able to reach you.
- Find a boating course in your area (Red Cross, U.S. Power Squadron, the U.S. Coast Guard Auxiliary, US Sailing, etc) -- these courses teach about navigation rules, emergency procedures and the effects of wind, water conditions, and weather.
- Watch the weather: Know local weather conditions and prepare for electrical storms. Watch local news programs. Stop boating as soon as you see or hear a storm.

Home Pools
- Learn to swim. The best thing anyone can do to stay safe in and around the water is to learn to swim--this includes adults and children. The American Red Cross has swimming courses for people of any age and swimming

ability. To enroll in a course to learn or improve your ability to swim, contact your local Red Cross chapter.
- Never leave a child unobserved around water. Your eyes must be on the child at all times. Adult supervision is recommended.
- Install a phone by the pool or keep a cordless phone nearby so that you can call 9-1-1 in an emergency.
- Learn Red Cross CPR and insist that babysitters, grandparents, and others who care for your child know CPR.
- Post CPR instructions and 9-1-1 or your local emergency number in the pool area.
- Enclose the pool completely with a self-locking, self-closing fence with vertical bars. Openings in the fence should be no more than four inches wide. If the house is part of the barrier, the doors leading from the house to the pool should remain locked and be protected with an alarm that produces sounds when the door is unexpectedly opened.
- Never leave furniture near the fence that would enable a child to climb over the fence.
- Always keep basic lifesaving equipment by the pool and know how to use it. Pole, rope, and personal flotation devices (PFDs) are recommended.
- Keep toys away from the pool when it is not in use. Toys can attract young children into the pool.
- Pool covers should always be completely removed prior to pool use.
- To learn more about home pool safety, you can purchase the video *It Only Takes a Minute* from your local Red Cross chapter.
- If a child is missing, check the pool first. Go to the edge of the pool and scan the entire pool, bottom, and surface, as well as the surrounding pool area.

Keeping Children Safe In, On, and Around the Water

- Maintain constant supervision. Watch children around any water environment (pool, stream, lake, tub, toilet, bucket of water), no matter what skills your child has acquired and no matter how shallow the water.
- Don't rely on substitutes. The use of flotation devices and inflatable toys **cannot** replace parental supervision. Such devices could suddenly shift position, lose air, or slip out from underneath, leaving the child in a dangerous situation.
- Enroll children in a water safety course or Learn to Swim program. Your decision to provide your child with an early aquatic experience is a gift that will have infinite rewards. These courses encourage safe practices. You can also purchase a *Community Water Safety* manual at your local Red Cross.
- Parents should take a CPR course. Knowing these skills can be important around the water and you will expand your capabilities in providing care for your child. You can contact your local Red Cross to enroll in a CPR for Infants and Child course.
- Select a supervised area. A trained lifeguard who can help in an emer-

gency is the best safety factor. Even good swimmers can have an unexpected medical emergency in the water. Never swim alone.

Lakes and Rivers
- Learn to swim. The best thing anyone can do to stay safe in and around the water is to learn to swim--this includes adults and children. The American Red Cross has swimming courses for people of any age and swimming ability. To enroll in swim course, contact your <u>local Red Cross chapter</u>.
- Select a supervised area. A trained lifeguard who can help in an emergency is the best safety factor. Even good swimmers can have an unexpected medical emergency in the water. Never swim alone.
- Select an area that is clean and well maintained. A clean bathhouse, clean restrooms, and a litter-free environment show the management's concern for your health and safety.
- Select an area that has good water quality and safe natural conditions. Murky water, hidden underwater objects, unexpected drop-offs, and aquatic plant life are hazards. Water pollution can cause health problems for swimmers. Strong tides, big waves, and currents can turn an event that began as fun into a tragedy.
- Make sure the water is deep enough before entering headfirst. Too many swimmers are seriously injured every year by entering headfirst into water that is too shallow. A feet first entry is much safer than diving.
- Be sure rafts and docks are in good condition. A well-run open-water facility maintains its rafts and docks in good condition, with no loose boards or exposed nails. Never swim under a raft or dock. Always look before jumping off a dock or raft to be sure no one is in the way.
- Avoid drainage ditches and arroyos. Drainage ditches and arroyos for water run-off are not good places for swimming or playing in the water. After heavy rains, they can quickly change into raging rivers that can easily take a human life. Even the strongest swimmers are no match for the power of the water. Fast water and debris in the current make ditches and arroyos very dangerous.

Waterparks
- Learn to swim. The best thing anyone can do to stay safe in and around the water is to learn to swim--this includes adults and children. The American Red Cross has swimming courses for people of any age and swimming ability. To enroll in a swim course, contact your <u>local Red Cross chapter</u>.
- Select a supervised area. A trained lifeguard who can help in an emergency is the best safety factor. Even good swimmers can have an unexpected medical emergency in the water. Never swim alone.
- Read all posted signs. Follow the rules and directions given by lifeguards. Ask questions I f you are not sure about a correct procedure.
- When you go from one attraction to another, note that the water depth may be different and that the attraction should be used in a different way.

- Before you start down a water slide, get in the correct position -- face up and feet first.
- Some facilities provide life jackets at no charge. If you cannot swim, wear a Coast Guard-approved life jacket. Check others in your group as well.

Ocean Safety
- Learn to swim. The best thing anyone can do to stay safe in and around the water is to learn to swim--this includes adults and children. The American Red Cross has swimming courses for people of any age and swimming ability. Contact your <u>local Red Cross chapter</u> for information on courses.
- Stay within the designated swimming area, ideally within the visibility of a lifeguard.
- Select a supervised area. A trained lifeguard who can help in an emergency is the best safety factor. Even good swimmers can have an unexpected medical emergency in the water. Never swim alone.
- Check the surf conditions **before** you enter the water. Check to see if a warning flag is up or check with a lifeguard for water conditions, beach conditions, or any potential hazards.
- Stay away from piers, pilings, and diving platforms when in the water.
- Keep a lookout for aquatic life. Water plants and animals may be dangerous. Avoid patches of plants. Leave animals alone.
- Make sure you always have enough energy to swim back to shore.
- Don't try to swim against a current if caught in one. Swim gradually out of the current, by swimming across it.

Personal Watercraft (Jet Skis)
- Learn to swim. The best thing anyone can do to stay safe in and around the water is to learn to swim. This includes anyone participating in any water sport or boating activity. The American Red Cross has swimming courses for people of any age and swimming ability. To enroll in a swim course, contact your <u>local Red Cross chapter</u>.
- Know your local laws and regulations. Some states have special laws governing the use of personal water craft (PWC) which address operations, registration and licensing requirements, education, required safety equipment and minimum ages.
- Operate your PWC with courtesy and common sense. Follow the traffic pattern of the waterway. Obey no-wake and speed zones.
- Use extreme caution around swimmers and surfers. Run your PWC at a slow speed until the craft is away from shore, swimming areas, and docks. Avoid passing close to other boats and jumping wakes. This behavior is dangerous and often illegal.
- Coast Guard-approved life jackets should be worn by the operator of the PWC as well as any riders.
- Ride with a buddy. PWCs should always travel in groups of two or three. You never know when an emergency might occur.

- Alcohol and operating a PWC doesn't mix. Alcohol impairs your judgment, balance, and coordination. For the same reasons it is dangerous to operate an automobile, people should not operate a boat or PWC while drinking alcohol.

Sail boarding and Windsurfing
- Always wear a Coast Guard-approved life jacket.
- Wear a wet suit in cold water to prevent hypothermia.
- You need good physical strength and swimming ability. The American Red Cross has swimming courses for people of any age and swimming ability. To enroll in a swim course, contact your local Red Cross chapter.
- Take windsurfing lessons from a qualified instructor.
- Know local weather conditions. Make sure the water and weather conditions are safe. Because water conducts electricity, it is wise to stop swimming, boating or any activities on the water as soon as you see or hear a storm. Also, heavy rains can make certain areas dangerous.
- Select a supervised area. A trained lifeguard who can help in an emergency is the best safety factor. Even good swimmers can have an unexpected medical emergency in the water. Never swim alone.

Skin and SCUBA Diving
- Receive instructions/take lessons from qualified divers before participating.
- Get a medical examination and take a swim test before learning SCUBA diving.
- Once certified, do not dive in rough or dangerous waters or in environments for which you are not trained. Ice, cave, and shipwreck diving require special training. One can easily get lost or trapped and run out of air.
- Never dive by yourself.
- Learn to swim. The best thing anyone can do to stay safe in and around the water is to learn to swim. This includes anyone participating in any water sport. The American Red Cross has swimming courses for people of any age and swimming ability. To enroll in a swim course, contact your local Red Cross chapter.
- Know local weather conditions. Make sure the water and weather conditions are safe. Because water conducts electricity, it is wise to stop swimming, boating or any activities on the water as soon as you see or hear a storm. Also, heavy rains can make certain areas dangerous.

Snorkeling
- Practice in shallow water.
- Check the equipment carefully and know how it functions.
- Learn how to clear water from the snorkel.
- Learn how to put your mask back on when you tread water.

- Be careful not to swim or be carried by a current too far from shore or the boat.
- Select a supervised area. A trained lifeguard who can help in an emergency is the best safety factor. Even good swimmers can have an unexpected medical emergency in the water. Never swim alone.
- Learn to swim. The best thing anyone can do to stay safe in and around the water is to learn to swim. This includes anyone participating in any water sport. The American Red Cross has swimming courses for people of any age and swimming ability. To enroll in a swim course, contact your local Red Cross chapter.
- Know local weather conditions. Make sure the water and weather conditions are safe. Because water conducts electricity, it is wise to stop swimming, boating or any activities on the water as soon as you see or hear a storm. Also, heavy rains can make certain areas dangerous.

Surfing
- Take lessons from an experienced individual.
- Wear a wet suit when in cold water.
- Never surf alone. Select a supervised area. A trained lifeguard who can help in an emergency is the best safety factor. Even good swimmers can have an unexpected medical emergency in the water.
- Learn to swim. The best thing anyone can do to stay safe in and around the water is to learn to swim. This includes anyone participating in any water sport. The American Red Cross has swimming courses for people of any age and swimming ability. To enroll in a swim course, contact your local Red Cross chapter.
- Know local weather conditions. Make sure the water and weather conditions are safe. Because water conducts electricity, it is wise to stop swimming, boating or any activities on the water as soon as you see or hear a storm. Also, heavy rains can make certain areas dangerous

Tubing and Rafting
- Always wear a Coast Guard-approved life jacket.
- Do not overload the raft.
- Do not go rafting after a heavy rain.
- When rafting with a tour company, make sure the guides are qualified. Check with the local chamber of commerce for listings of accredited tour guides and companies.
- Learn to swim. The best thing anyone can do to stay safe in and around the water is to learn to swim. This includes anyone participating in any water sport. The American Red Cross has swimming courses for people of any age and swimming ability. To enroll in a swim course, contact your local Red Cross chapter.
- Know local weather conditions. Make sure the water and weather conditions are safe. Because water conducts electricity, it is wise to stop swim-

ming, boating, or any activities on the water as soon as you see or hear a storm. Also, heavy rains can make certain areas dangerous.
- Select a supervised area. A trained lifeguard who can help in an emergency is the best safety factor. Even good swimmers can have an unexpected medical emergency in the water. Never swim alone.
- American Red Cross, National Headquarters website.
- http://www.redcross.org

GENERAL SAFETY CONSIDERATIONS

It is important that all people whether or not they normally participate in aquatic activities, understand what is involved in water safety. Water safety knowledge and skills provide the foundation for which all aquatic activity should be based. Prevention is always better than care. In the aquatic environment, this means that preventing water accidents by taking precautions is better than having to be rescued.
- Establish clear gestures for emergency situations. Use printed material to add any verbal information that may be needed, especially safety precautions.
- Keep the deck and pool area free of clutter. Provide clear pathways (at least 3 feet wide) to and from all areas of the facility. Be sure safety lines are in place securely. Have auditory and visual signals that mean stop, stand still and danger.
- Have large prints of rules also available in case they are needed.
- Create clear observation points for staff use.
- Post easy to read maps indicating emergency exits to the outside.
- Put down mats in areas that are prone to slip and fall accidents (wet areas, pool, whirlpool, steam areas, etc.).
- Use preactivity screening to head off risk factors at the outset.
- Have all instructions and emergency action procedures available by all phones.
- Encourage adult participants to help each other by teaching them support positions and how to help a person to recover from a float or glide.
- Diving is prohibited for people with atlantoaxial instability. This condition of an unstable vertebrae is sometimes found in people with Down's syndrome. Diving should not be permitted with these individuals unless a medical release says that cervical X rays confirm a normal spine. You must make sure that these individuals are well suited for water activities.
- Do not hesitate to use time out procedures or to stop any activity of anyone if the participant(s) cannot control their behavior.
- Avoid activities that may cause skin abrasions. If a person has a lower back instability (such as paralysis or spina bifida), they should be prohibited from diving and/or any other activity that may cause a twisting of the spine.
- Participants should not be allowed to become chilled or fatigued while

in the water. Each person should know his/her own limitations and this should be their comfort guide in the water. If the person has a seizure in the water, help that individual immediately. Individuals who have seizures and that are not under medical supervision will need close supervision and they should probably swim only in shallower waters.

Safety must not be taken lightly. One serious accident can permanently disable a person, destroy a person's professional career and create a lifetime of guilt. Water safety is an essential theme in a well balanced learn to swim program. Water safety education involves making sure that all those who are involved in activities in, on or near the water understand how to behave in a safe manner. These individuals should also have some basic knowledge of how to help others having difficulty in the aquatic environment. It is vital that water safety is included in all learn to swim programs from the beginning and continues through the duration of the lessons.

RISK MANAGEMENT

Risk management is identifying, analyzing and evaluating risks that may affect an individual and how one would devise a plan to minimize or eliminate any and all risks. The primary goal and objective of risk management is for the safety of the participants. Participants expect and deserve a safe and healthy aquatic environment. If it is not safe, your participants may become distracted, be afraid to participate or even be at the risk for some type of injury. In addition to your participants getting injured, you have to look out for yourself. You must be aware of all dangerous and/or hazardous situations because if you fail to see them this could cause some major distractions and even injuries. You should know the requirements for your local, state and federal agencies in regards to safety practices and policies. Regardless of whether or not there is a regulation you have the deciding vote in the safety of your participants. It is up to you to decide what is right for all individuals involved.

The most effective risk management programs begin with your awareness that risks may occur and they are usually present. Safety awareness is vital and a necessity for recognizing risks so that the condition(s) may be controlled or even eliminated. Just remember risk management involves always being well prepared and having the attitude of watchfulness and safety. The more you do in order to make the learning environment safe, the more your participants and you will benefit.

All instructors are assumed to be competent to lead their respective activities. The definition of competent or competency may appear to be difficult. The United States Court System defines competent as a reasonable and prudent professional utilizing the best and most current professional practices. This is also known as the standard of care. In order to be considered competent the instructor must be able to show that a standard of care is comparable with that of the best professional practices being followed.

Standard of care should look at general supervision of your area and this may include awareness of dangerous situations, knowledge of first aid and CPR and communications with the students and their parents. Te students must also understand and adhere to the pool rules and regulations. Your activity must provide adequate instructions and progressions being taught. You must understand your students including their age, ability, maturity and any other special situations that may need to be noted such as a physical disability. You must warn the students of any potential dangers in the aquatic environment around you.

You must understand the aquatic environment around you including the equipment. The equipment, the pool water and the aquatic structures must be constantly checked and maintained safely. If everything is carefully monitored and maintained, the instructor has a better chance of proving to be competent.

GUIDE TO SAFETY TIPS IN THE AQUATIC ENVIRONMENT

The Unites States Lifesaving Association

1. **Swim Near A Lifeguard:** USLA statistics over a ten year period show that the chance of drowning at a beach without lifeguard protection is almost five times as great as drowning at a beach with lifeguards. USLA has calculated the chance that a person will drown while attending a beach protected by USLA affiliated lifeguards at 1 in 18 million (.0000055%).
2. **Learn To Swim:** Learning to swim is the best defense against drowning. Teach children to swim at an early age. Children who are not taught when they are very young tend to avoid swim instruction as they age, probably due to embarrassment. Swimming instruction is a crucial step to protecting children from injury or death.
3. **Never Swim Alone:** Many drownings involve single swimmers. When you swim with a buddy, if one of you has a problem, the other may be able to help, including signaling for assistance from others. At least have someone onshore watching you.
4. **Don't Fight the Current:** USLA has found that some 80% of rescues by USLA affiliated lifeguards at ocean beaches are caused by rip currents. These currents are formed by surf and gravity, because once surf pushes water up the slope of the beach, gravity pulls it back. This can create concentrated rivers of water moving offshore. Some people mistakenly call this an undertow, but there is no undercurrent, just an offshore current. If you are caught in a rip current, don't fight it by trying to swim directly to shore. Instead, swim parallel to shore until you feel the current relax, then swim to shore. Most rip currents are narrow and a short swim parallel to shore will bring you to safety.
5. **Swim Sober:** Alcohol is a major factor in drowning. Alcohol can reduce body temperature and impair swimming ability. Perhaps more impor-

tantly, both alcohol and drugs impair good judgement, which may cause people to take risks they would not otherwise take.
6. **Leash Your Board:** Surfboards and bodyboards should be used only with a leash. Leashes are usually attached to the board and the ankle or wrist. They are available in most shops where surfboards and bodyboards are sold or rented. With a leash, the user will not become separated from the floatation device. One additional consideration is a breakaway leash. A few drownings have been attributed to leashes becoming entangled in underwater obstructions. A breakaway leash avoids this problem.
7. **Don't Float Where You Can't Swim:** Nonswimmers often use floatation devices, like inflatable rafts, to go offshore. If they fall off, they can quickly drown. No one should use a floatation device unless they are able to swim. Use of a leash is not enough because a non-swimmer may panic and be unable to swim back to the floatation device, even with a leash. The only exception is a person wearing a Coast Guard approved life jacket.
8. **Life Jackets = Boating Safety:** Some 80% of fatalities associated with boating accidents are from drowning. Most involve people who never expected to end up in the water, but fell overboard or ended up in the water when the boat sank. Children are particularly susceptible to this problem and in many states, children are required to be in lifejackets whenever they are aboard boats.
9. **Don't Dive Headfirst, Protect Your Neck:** Serious, lifelong injuries, including paraplegia, occur every year due to diving headfirst into unknown water and striking the bottom. Bodysurfing can result in a serious neck injury when the swimmer's neck strikes the bottom. Check for depth and obstructions before diving, then go in feet first the first time; and use caution while bodysurfing, always extending a hand ahead of you.
10. **At Home, You're the Lifeguard:** Drowning is the leading cause of accidental death in many states for children age one and two. A major reason for this is home pools, which can be death traps for toddlers. Many of these deaths occur in the few moments it takes a parent to answer a telephone or doorbell. NEVER leave a child alone anywhere near a pool. Make sure it is completely fenced, that the fence is locked, and that there is no access from the home to the pool. Don't let your child or a neighbor's child get into the pool when you're not there.

Heat and Cold Related Emergencies

A person can get sick/ill from hot or cold temperatures even if they do not seem to be extreme. The human body is equipped to withstand extremes of temperature, both hot and cold. The illness a person gets will depend on the likelihood of these factors: physical activity, clothing, wind, humidity, working and living conditions, a person's age and state of health. The body temperature must remain constant for the body to work efficiently.

People who are at risk for Heat or Cold Emergencies:
- those who work / exercise strenuously outdoors
- elderly people
- young children
- those with health problems
- those who have had heat/cold related problems in the past
- those who have cardiovascular disease or any other condition that can or will cause poor circulation
- those who take medications to eliminate water from the body (diuretics)

Heat Related Emergencies:

All of these conditions are due to overexposure to the heat. Heat cramps are the least severe, but they can be a signal to the person that the body is being taken over by the heat.

Heat Cramps: Muscle spasms that are painful. It could be a warning sign or signal of a heat related emergency. They usually occur in the legs or abdominal region.

<u>Treatment</u>: Rest the victim in a cold place. Give him/her cool water. Do not give the victim salt tablets or salt water.

Heat Exhuastion: More severe that heat cramps. It will usually occur after a long period of strenuous exercise or work in the heat and/or humidity.

<u>Signs/Symptoms</u>: normal or below normal body temperature   nausea

Cool, moist, pale or red skin   weakness exhaustion

Headache   dizziness

<u>Treatment</u>: Rest in a cool place and give him / her cool water.

Heat Stroke: Least common heat emergency, but it is the most severe. It usually occurs after the signals of heat exhaustion are ignored. The body systems begin to fail.

<u>Signs/Symptoms</u>: red, hot, dry skin   change in consciousness

Rapid, weak pulse   rapid, shallow breathing

<u>Treatment</u>: Follow these step immediately:
1. Get the victim out of the heat
2. Cool the body with cool wet clothes, such as towels and loosen all tight clothing

3. If conscious, give cool water to drink (but not too rapidly)
4. Minimize shock
5. Call EMS

Cold Related Emergencies:

Hypothermia: When the body can no longer generate enough heat to maintain normal body temperature, it is a general cooling off of the body. The air temperature does not have to be below freezing for hypothermia to develop. Wind and humidity have some control over the body's ability to control its temperature. Anyone who remains in colder water or wet clothing for an extended period of time may develop hypothermia. Medical conditions (infection), diabetes, stroke and drinking alcohol are other things that can affect the body's ability to maintain normal body temperature.

<u>Signs/Symptoms:</u> shivering (could be absent in later stages)   numbness

Slow, irregular pulse   glassy stare

Apathy   decreased levels of consiousness

<u>Treatment</u>: Call EMS. Remove any wet clothing and dry the victim. Gradually warm up the body with blankets and dry clothing and moving him/her to a dry environment. Do NOT warm the victim too quickly as this can lead to heart problems. Monitor vital signs and wait for EMS.

Frostbite: Freezing of body parts exposed to the cold. The air temperature, the wind speed and the length of exposure are all things to look at when discussing frostbite. Water will freeze in and between the body's cells. Frostbite can cause loss of fingers, hands, arms, toes, feet and legs.

<u>Signs/Symptoms</u>: lack of feeling in affected area

Skin that appears waxy   skin that is cold to the touch

Discolored skin   (flushed - white – yellow - blue)

<u>Treatment</u>: Warm the area gently. Never rub that area as it can cause further damage. Gradually warm the affected area in water 100-105 degrees Fahrenheit. The affected part should not touch the bottom or the side of the container. Keep the affected area in the water until it is red and warm to the touch. Bandage the area with a dry, sterile dressing. If the affected area is the toes or fingers place gauze between them and get medical attention as soon as possible.

Hazardous Weather

The weather and the environment could be factors to consider when working in an outdoor aquatic facility or when dealing with any outdoor activities.

These conditions could vary greatly in different parts of the United States. This information is to be used as a guide and an incentive to seek out and develop local resources that can provide specific information and / or training needed.

Certain cloud formations are associated with change in weather. By becoming familiar with these you can often know when weather is likely to change. Clouds that are high and hazy usually form a halo around the sun or moon. These clouds indicate that a storm may arrive within an hour. Large clouds with cauliflower like tops indicate an immediate thunderstorm. These clouds will look dark and heavy from below when they are about to erupt. Rolling dark clouds indicate that bad weather can arrive within minutes. Fleecy white clouds indicate good weather is ahead. Lightning behavior is random and unpredictable. It is recommended that a very conservative attitude towards it be taken. Preparedness and quick responses are the best defense towards any lightning hazard.

Once a storm or other bad weather is predicted or seen, you should start looking for other signs, such as lightning or thunder. Estimating the distance to a storm is easy. When you see lightning, count until you hear thunder and divide that number by five, to estimate the storm in miles. There are no guidelines for determining exactly when the water should be cleared of swimmers because of an impending storm. A safe practice would be to clear the water when the lightning is seen or thunder is heard. A recommended time should be until at least thirty minutes after the last blast of thunder is heard or lightning is seen. Guidelines should be established on how to respond to thunder and lightning and they should be practiced to assure the safety of the patrons.

Lightning causes more deaths annually in the United States than any other weather hazard, including blizzards, hurricanes, floods, tornadoes, earthquakes and volcanic eruptions. The National Weather Service estimates lightning kills nearly 100 people annually and injures an additional 300. Lightning occurs when particles of water and ice inside storm clouds lose electrons. Eventually the cloud becomes divided into layers of positive and negative particles. Most electrical currents run between the layers inside the cloud. However, occasionally the negative charge flashes toward the ground, which has a positive charge. An electrical current snakes back and forth between the ground and the cloud many times in the second that we see a flash of lightning. Anything tall - a tower, a tree or person will become a path for the electrical current.

Traveling at speeds up to 300 miles per second, a lightning strike can hurt a person through the air, burn his or her clothes off and sometimes cause the heart to stop beating. The most severe lightning strike carries up to 50 million volts of electricity, enough to keep 13,000 homes running. Lightning can flash over a person's body, or in the most dangerous path, it can travel through the blood vessels and nerves before it reaches the ground. Besides burns, lightning can also cause damage to the body in a means such as loss of hearing, fractures and possibly even loss of eyesight. The victim sometimes acts confused and may describe the episode as getting hit in the head or hearing an explosion.

Use common sense around thunderstorms. If you see a storm approaching

do not wait until it is too late to seek shelter. If a thunderstorm threatens, The National Weather Service advises the following:
- go inside a building or a home
- stop swimming as water conducts electricity
- stay away from the telephone unless it is an emergency
- stay away from tall trees and telephone poles if outside
- stay off hilltops, try to crouch down in a ravine or valley
- go inside a car and roll up the windows
- avoid wire fences and anything else that may conduct electricity

Tornado Procedures

Tornadoes are nature's most violent storms, and over a small area are the most destructive. A tornado's whirling winds may reach 300 miles an hour or more. Generally short lived and fast moving, they can level whole city blocks in a matter of seconds. Damage or destruction of facilities and equipment at your site, and the loss of vital records may result in significant economic loss and disruption of operations for a long period of time. The National Weather Service is responsible for issuing weather warnings to the public. A tornado watch means that the conditions are right for tornadoes to develop. A tornado warning means that a tornado has been sighted in the area. Develop procedures for response to a tornado threat that may affect your facility

You must first use some kind of notification and warning system. How is this notification received, by what means? Most places now utilize sirens to inform the public of an impending tornado. When a watch or warning is issued you must follow your plan, in addition to continuously monitoring the weather. In the situation of a watch the pools may want to be cleared. It is better to be safe than sorry. In the case of a warning shelter must be taken. The tornado shelter needs of each site will vary according to the size and type of facility involved and the size of the organization. It is usually recommended that 5-6 square feet per person be recommended for adults.

Before you determine the location of your shelters you must look for and record the location of the following:
- site equipment and other debris
- ground embankment against the buildings
- mechanical equipment on the roof
- electrical service entrance
- changes in roof level

Take a long look from each direction and notify building entrances, windows and construction facilities.

The best areas to consider for your shelter are:
- the lowest floor
- interior spaces, no walls on the exterior
- basement
- any area of the building with rigid structural frames

You want to avoid any area near windows or skylights. You should also avoid interior locations where interior doors swing. When the storm hits the doors are likely to swing violently. Often the best available shelter spaces in a building cannot be occupied during emergencies for various reasons. You must make sure you have adequate shelter available in the case of a tornado emergency. Once an area has been established for all parts of the facility you must include a diagram and map out all exits and safety areas.

Earthquake Procedures

1. Remain calm
2. Immediately clear the pool. Ask patrons and staff to: Stand next to major walls or in a doorway; and stay away from large windows.
3. If you are outdoors during the initial quake, clear outdoor pools. Ask patrons to stay away from buildings, utility poles and power lines.
4. After the initial quake, immediately begin a building evacuation. Be prepared to handle any first aid situation from fire, gas or chlorine leaks.
5. After shocks are very common after the initial quake.
6. Communication lines and wires may be down so try to find a way to get the help you need.
7. If available, use a battery operated radio to keep updated on any further news or happenings.
8. Keep a log of events to help you accurately fill out any necessary incident and/or accident reports.

Do not leave the facility until it is secured and all the emergency situations have been addressed; or you have been given permission to leave the area.

EXPOSURE CONTROL PLAN

For Compliance with OSAHA Standard for Bloodborne Pathogens

In December 1991, The Occupational Safety and Health Administration (OSHA) issued a BLOODBORNE pathogens standard to protect US workers and help prevent deaths and infection, which occur each year due to BLOODBORNE pathogens.

BLOODBORNE pathogens are microorganisms in human blood that can cause disease in humans. They include the hepatitis B virus (HBGV) and the human immunodeficiency virus (HIV), which causes AIDS. The occupational transmission of HIV is relatively rare but the lethal nature of HIV requires that every possible precaution is taken to prevent exposure.

The standard mandates that employers must institute engineering controls, work practices, personal protective equipment and employee training programs that will reduce risks for all employees expose to blood. The greatest BLOODBORNE risk workers face is the threat of infection posed by the hepatitis B virus. It is estimated that roughly 6,000 to 7,400 cases of HBV due to occupational exposure occur each year.

Below is a summary of the key provisions of the final standard.

PURPOSE: The purpose of this standard is to limit occupational exposure to blood and other potential infectious materials. These exposures could result in the transmission of BLOODBORNE pathogens, which could lead to disease of death.

SCOPE: The standard covers ALL EMPLOYEES who, as a result of performing their job duties, could come in contact with blood or other potentially infectious materials. OSHA does not list all occupations where exposures could occur. OSHA indicates that "good Samaritan" acts usually don not fall under this standard as occupational exposure. Infectious materials include semen, vaginal secretions, cerebrospinal fluid, synovial fluid, pleural fluid, pericardial fluid, peritoneal fluid, amniotic fluid, saliva in dental procedures, an body fluid visibly contaminated with blood and all body fluids in situations where it is difficult or impossible to differentiate between body fluids. Other infectious materials include HIV or HBV containing bodily tissues.

EXPOSURE CONTROL PLAN: The exposure control plan is a written plan identifying tasks and procedures, and job classifications where occupational exposure to blood may occur, without regard to personal protective clothing and equipment. It must outline a schedule for implementation of the standard and specify the procedure for evaluation circumstances surrounding exposure incidents.

This plan must be accessible to all employees and available to OSHA. This plan must be reviewed and updated annually, if necessary.

METHODS OF COMPLIANCE: The standard mandates the use of universal precautions, with an emphasis of engineering control and established work place practices. The standard requires employers to provide facilities to employees for had washing following exposure to blood. The standard includes procedures to minimize needle sticks, minimize splashing and spraying of blood, ensure appropriate procedures of shipping and disposing of contaminated waste.

The standard requires that an employer provide, at no cost to the employee appropriate personal protective equipment such as gloves, gowns, masks, mouthpieces, etc.

HEPATITIS B VACCINATIONS: The standard requires vaccinations be made available to all employees who have occupational exposure to blood with in 10 working days of assignments, at no cost. Employees must sign a declination form if they choose not to be vaccinated, but may later opt to receive the vaccine at no cost to the employee.

POST- EXPOSURE AND FOLLOW-UP: The standard specifies procedures to be made available to all employees who have had an exposure incident. Any laboratory tests must be conducted by an accredited laboratory at no cost to the employee. Follow- up must include confidential medical evaluation documenting the circumstances of exposure, employee's blood if he/she consents, and counseling and evaluation.

HAZARD COMMUNICATIONS: The standard requires warning labels including the orange and orange-red biohazard symbol be affixed to containers of regulated waste, refrigerators and freezers and other containers which are used to store or transport blood or other potentially infectious materials. Red bags or containers may be used instead of labeling. When a facility uses universal precautions, labeling is not required, and regulated waste, which has been decontaminated, need not be labeled.

INFORMATION AND TRANING: The standard requires training within 90 days of effective date of this standard initially upon assignment and annually. Training must include making accessible a copy of the standard and an explanation of its contents, discussion of BLOODBORNE diseases and their transmission, exposure control plan, work place practices and personal protective clothing, an emergency procedures involving blood.

RECORD KEEPING: The standard requires medical records be kept for each employee with occupational exposure for the duration of employment plus 30 years. Training records must be maintained for three years and must include dates, contents of the training program or a summary, trainer's name and qualifications, names and job titles of all persons attending the session.

DATES TO REMEMBER: The effective date of the standard is 90 days after publication. Exposure control plan must be completed within 60 days of effective date. Information and training requirements take effect 90 days following the effective date. All other provisions of the standard take effect 120 days after effective date.

EXAMPLES OF EXPOSURE PLAN

-Name of Facility-

BLOODBORNE PATHOGENS EXPOSURE CONTROL PLAN
For compliance with OSHA Standard for Bloodborne Pathogens

Prepared By

_____

Reviewed By

_____

Effective By

_____

In accordance with OSHA Bloodborne Pathogens Standard 29 CFR 1910.1030, the following exposure control plan has been developed. A copy of the standard and definitions relating to the exposure control plan is found in Appendix A.

EXPOSURE DETERMNATION OF JOB CLASSIFICATIONS:

1. This exposure control plan has identified the job classifications listed in Appendix B as those who could be exposed to bloodborne pathogens in the course of fulfilling their job requirements.
2. A list of tasks and procedures performed by those listed in the above classifications in which exposure to bloodborne pathogens may occur is required. This exposure determination shall be made without regard to the use of personal protective equipment. Task/procedures may include, but not limited to, these examples:
   a. Minor injuries that occur within a health club or fitness facility setting, i.e., bloody nose, minor scrapes, and minor cuts
   b. Initial care of injuries that requires medical attention, i.e., broken bones protruding through the skin, severe lacerations, etc.
   c. Care of injured person during a sport activity, i.e. basketball and tennis
   d. Care of members receiving testing, i.e. cholesterol screening with needles.
   e. Housekeeping tasks associated with body fluids or blood spills.

3. Universal precautions shall be observed in order to prevent contact with blood or other potentially infectious materials. All blood or other potentially contaminated body fluids shall be considered to be infectious.
4. Engineering and Work Practice Controls are designed to eliminate or minimize exposure. An exposure incident is defined as contact with blood or other potentially infectious materials. An exposure investigation form shall be completed each time an incident occurs.
5. Hand Washing: The facility shall provide hand-washing facilities, which are readily accessible. When provisions for hand washing are not feasible, the facility will provide either an antiseptic hand cleaner or antiseptic towelettes.

   Those exposed shall wash hands or any other skin with soap and water, or flush mucous membranes with water immediately or as soon as feasible following contacts of such body areas with blood or other potentially infectious materials.

   Employees shall wash their hands immediately or as soon as feasible after removal of gloves or other personal protective equipment.

6. Housekeeping and Waste Procedures: The facility shall ensure that the work site is maintained in a clean and sanitary condition. All equipment and materials shall be cleaned and decontaminated after contact with blood or other potentially infectious materials.

   Contaminated work surfaces shall be decontaminated with appropriate disinfectant immediately after completion of incident. Protective coverings such as plastic wrap, aluminum foil or imperviously backed absorbent paper used to cover equipment and environmental surfaces, shall be removed and replaced as soon as feasible when they become contaminated with blood or other potentially infectious materials.

   All receptacles intended for reuse having a reasonable likelihood for becoming contaminated with blood or other potentially infectious materials shall be inspected and decontaminated on a regularly scheduled basis and cleaned and decontaminated immediately or as soon as feasible upon visible contamination.

   Materials used in the treatment of blood spills that are soaked or caked with blood shall be bagged, tied and designated as a biohazard. The bag shall then be removed from the site as soon as feasible and replaced with a clean bag. In this facility, bags designated, as biohazard shall be in red color and labeled with a biohazard label and shall be located

The housekeeping staff shall respond immediately to any major blood or other potentially infectious materials incident so that it can be cleaned, decontaminated and removed immediately. Broken glass shall not be picked up directly with the hands. It shall be cleaned up using mechanical means, such as a brush and a dustpan. Broken glass shall be containerized.

Contaminated sharp objects such as needles or broken glass shall be placed into appropriate sharp containers. The containers shall be maintained in an upright position. These containers shall be easily accessible for the immediate disposal of needles or sharp objects.

Disposal of all regulated waste shall be in accordance with applicable regulations of the United States, States and Territories, and political subdivisions of States and Territories.

7. Procedures: All procedures involving blood or other potentially infectious materials shall be performed in such a manner as to minimize splashing, spraying, splattering, and generation of droplets of these substances.
8. If facility has its own laundry, contaminated laundry shall be handled as little as possible with a minimum of agitation. Gloves must be worn when handling contaminated laundry. If no on-site laundry facility, the contaminated laundry shall be bagged or containerized and marked as biohazard. They should be sent to a commercial establishment approved for cleaning biohazard material.
9. Personal Protective Equipment: Gloves shall be worn when it can be reasonably anticipated that there may be hand contact with blood. Disposable gloves shall be used in all situations, and may not be reused.

    Masks, combination with eye protection devices, such as goggles or glasses shall be worn whenever splashes may be generated. Other appropriate protective clothing shall be made available, such as gowns, aprons, lab coats, etc.

    Appropriate personal protective equipment shall be readily accessible at the work site. Workers can find personal protective equipment in the following locations:

10. Hepatitis B Vaccination

    Hepatitis B vaccine shall be made available for workers in accordance with the standard, whose job assignment entails contact with blood or bodily fluids.

    The Hepatitis B vaccine shall be made available. Should the workers decline, a declination statement shall be signed. If an employee declines the Hepatitis B Vaccination, but at a later date while still covered under the standard decides to attempt the vaccination, the facility shall make available the Hepatitis B vaccine at that time.

The Hepatitis B vaccine shall be provided to those unvaccinated employees whose primary job assignment is NOT rendering of first aid ONLY in the case that they render assistance in any situation involving the presence of blood or other potentially infectious material.

The exposure incident investigation form must be used to report these incidents, in order for proper determination be made for the offering of Hepatitis B vaccine.

The full Hepatitis B vaccination series shall be made available as soon as possible, but in no event later than 24 hours, to all unvaccinated first aid providers who have rendered assistance in any situation in which there was possible exposure. The Hepatitis B vaccination record or declination statement shall be completed.

11. POST EXPOSURE EVALUATION AND FOLLOW UP: Following a report of an exposure incident, the facility shall make immediately available to the exposed employees a confidential medical examination and follows up, including all the elements included in this standard.
12. EMPLOYEE TRAINING AND RECORD KEEPING: The facility shall ensure that all employees whose job assignment may lead to occupational exposure participate in an awareness program, which includes all elements outlined in this standard.

The facility shall establish and maintain accurate medical records for each employee with occupational exposure. The record shall include all the elements outlined in this standard.

Training records must be maintained in accordance with this standard.

Chapter 8

∞

ADAPTED AQUATICS

THE quality of a civilization may be best judged by the way it treats its less fortunate members (Pearl S. Buck). Some parents of students with disabilities could not understand why their children had to be bussed to separate schools or place in special education classrooms. While some were told that their children night eventually move into regular programs once they met some prerequisite requirements, the reality was that this rarely if ever happened. Parents and advocates argued that students with disabilities should not have to earn their way into regular schools and regular classrooms.

Inclusion is a philosophy that supports placement of all students with disabilities in their neighborhood school (that they would attend if they did not have a disability), in regular education classrooms. Special education and other services are brought to the student while in regular education rather than having the student to these services in separate classes. Inclusion is a complex issue that has been interpreted differently by different people (Sherrill, 1998). Others (those who favor a more moderate view of inclusion or least restrictive environment) support the idea that, to receive an appropriate education, some students with disabilities might have to spend part of the day in alternative placements such as the resource room or in the community. However, some advocate that students with disabilities start their school day in a regular classroom with same age peers and are viewed as a member of the regular education class.

Inclusion is not dumping students with disabilities into regular education or regular physical education classes without support or forcing students to fit into existing curriculum designed for students without disabilities. All students with disabilities should be included in regular classes and welcomed by the regular physical education teacher and students without disabilities (Block, 1995). Because many schools are incorporating inclusion and mainstreaming into their curriculum, physical educators, especially those with no or minimal training in adapted physical education, now share the responsibility for teaching students with diverse abilities. Teachers should not assume that they always know the best way to perform a skill. Instead, they should, along with each student, adapt the movement form to the outcome of the task or goal. Adoption requires choices and strategies for individualization. Separate education is never equal education and all good physical education is adapted physical education (Paciorek&Jones, 1994).

The full inclusion concept may encourage physical educators to rethink the way teachers view teaching and to reflect on their professional sense of purpose. If physical educators are to embrace the value of including all children learning together in physical education settings, then meaningful relationships must be established with colleagues in the therapies and recreation and the parents of the children being taught The development of curriculum modifications in physical education and adaptations to methods are two ways in which to begin building such meaningful relationships. As inclusion becomes the way the whole school works, there will be many opportunities to develop equal status relationships. The future clearly challenges us to help children understand the fun, excitement, and opportunity afforded by diversity in the gymnasium, the school and the community, In the United Stated today, individuals with disabilities have a greater visibility than they did at any other time in history and this is mainly due to the The Americans with Disabilities Act pf 1990 (Rimmer. 1997). Doors that were once closed are beginning to open for people with special needs. This is only a beginning and with time and effort on our part, we can get these doors to stay open for everyone.

Mainstreaming means assigning the disabled to classes with the non disabled and providing successful and meaningful experiences for both, based on their abilities and needs. A clearer understanding of mainstreaming may be obtained if two additional items are included in the definition. The first item is concerned with the person's functioning ability or capability. Not all mentally or physically impaired people should be integrated into the regular classroom. Most educators admit that a continuum of services must be provided to the disabled, and to children functioning at lower learning levels, separate classes and/or schools may be the only alternative. The placement decision should be assessed on the child's ability. How well the person functions in an activity should be the standard for placement rather than a label such as emotionally or mentally impaired. A program should focus on the swimming ability rather than on the disability and this will permit more disabled individuals to participate in an aquatic program with the non disabled participants.

With a large segment of the population having varying degrees of disabilities, it is imperative that any and all means be utilized to assist the individual in their social functioning. Swimming offers some very unique opportunities to and for the disabled. Generally speaking, the values of swimming fall into three main categories: physiological, psychological and sociological (Amateur Swimming Association, 1989). There are few other sports which provide the opportunity for worthwhile and enjoyable participation for such a wide range of the community as does swimming. With few barriers to taking part, it is a lifelong activity and one that can be performed indoors or outdoors, dependent upon where you live.

Physiological benefits are subdivided into the organic (physical fitness) and the psychomotor (motor performance) areas. Organic development is divided further with four more components: cardiovascular endurance: muscle endurance: strength: and flexibility. Cardiovascular endurance is the ability of the heart, lung and circulatory system and its ability to handle and control vigorous activity. Muscle endurance is the capacity for the continued exertion and the ability of the muscle to sustain an activity for increased periods of time. Strength is the ability to exert force. And flexibility is it's defined as the ability to bend, stretch and move through the normal range of motion. The psychomotor area consists of speed, agility and perceptual motor factors. Speed is the ability to act or move quickly. Agility is the ability to change direction with controlled body movements. Perceptual motor factors have to do with balance, kinesthetic sense, laterally, dominance, spatial relationships. Directionality, visual and auditory discrimination, eye-hand –foot coordination. A well planned physical activity program will and should contribute to both the organic and the psychomotor development areas.

Psychological values are the same ones experienced by all individuals, regardless if they have a disability or not. The main value here is that of experiencing success. Everyone needs the opportunity to do something well and to enjoy the feeling of success. This is of special importance to individuals with impairments or disabilities. In a society structured for the non disabled, success is too often denied the person with a disability. A well planned aquatic activity can provide goals that are trainable for all. Opportunities for success should be a part of every aquatic experience.

Enhancing the individuals self image is the next concept to be stress in the aquatic environment. Being successful in any endeavor enhances the individuals self image and to a mentally impaired individual with limited academic ability, the success available through aquatics may be doubly important. Success increased the individuals regard for his/her worth and abilities, and it can also decree the emotional impact of the disability.

Providing positive emotional outlets is the third benefit seen in the psychological area. Swimming if fun and for some people it is one of the few play activities that they can engage in with relative ease. The aquatic program provides and environment in which anyone can release frustration safely. The water may be slapped, pushed, splashed and kicked and some individuals may wish to do so. It can be used us an emotional outlet.

The last benefit covered in this area is lessening the evidence of the disability. Much impairment is far less evident when the individual is in the water. Wheelchair users may be able to walk in the water depending upon their disability. Independent mobility is so often taken for granted by non disabled individuals and it can be a tremendous psychological boost for a disabled person. The advantage of buoyancy is the water facilitates many movements than are difficult or even impossible on land, thereby providing the individual with an opportunity to be less conscious of his/her disability. Many water safety skills can be performed as efficiently by some disabled peers as by non disabled ones, thus minimizing the apparent differences in land activities. This is the most important piece of the psychological area because it so often taken for granted.

Sociological values are stressed in the forms of peer group interaction, normalization and safety. The way the peer perceives us is important. Swimming can provide opportunities for peer group interaction, acceptance and learning of acceptable social behaviors such as sharing and waiting one's turn. Normalization is needed because categories and labels often serve to focus attention on impairments and disabilities rather than on the individual. Normalization has grown from the need to provide disabled people with the same experience as the non disabled. Within the range of his/her abilities. , every individual should be allowed the opportunity to function in the mainstream of society. Every effort should be made to give the individual as many normal experiences as possible, rather than having special programs become one way streets to further isolation. Swimming programs teach water adjustment, safety skills and swimming skill in whatever degree possible. They will also unquestionably enhance the safety of the individual and his/her family s they participate in any aquatic environment. This is a great social benefit and it should be the primary or main goal to any swimming program.

Interacting with the disabled individual in swimming programs can be both challenging and rewarding. It is not possible to name a single best teaching method or teaching strategy for this interaction. Individual differences in personalities and capabilities of both the student and the instructor must be recognized. Adequate planning can compensate for the limitation of either person. It is the instructor's responsibility to change or effectively neutralize all of the limitation (if possible). This can only be done when the instructor adequately assesses his/her own attitude and the needs of the student.

A key to all swimming programs should be to keep the fun in fundamental (this should be seen across the board in all physical education classes and activities). People like and will repeat something that is rewarding in some way: something that is fun and aquatics should serve this value for all individuals. The instructor should be award of the safety of all the participants and some modifications may need to be done. Utilized simple verbal directions; use visual cues and demonstrations, use encouragement and enthusiasm towards all participants and demonstrate patience, creativity and ingenuity. Essential factors to consider when selecting aquatic activity or game, evaluation and documentation of the participants progress; and reinforcement and carry over skills (VanDerveer, 1993). Focusing on abilities with respect for individual differences throughout the activity or game is important. One of the greatest dimensions about aquatic activities or games for the disabled is that when properly planned, they enhance the quality of life.

As education moves toward inclusive programming, all school activities need to be taken into account, curricular as well as extracurricular. Aside from an occasional weekend and excursion to special sports programs, athletic experiences for many people with disabilities are severely limited (Kozub, 1994). Often the opportunity to compete with others in interscholastic sports is available to typically developing students but not to those students with disabilities. The responsibility of obtaining an adequate level of skill (to participate in sports) should not rest totally on the individual with the disability. Communities need to distribute their resources equally to help provide all students with opportunities to compete on a regular basis. Games and sports should be bases on an athlete's personal attributes rather than on unnecessary administrative rules, coach's attitudes or other socially imposed barriers.

The area of aquatics offers great variety, including recreational swimming, survival and lifesaving skills, synchronized swimming, diving, water games, aquatic exercise, and competitive swimming (Vannier, 1977). The ability to swim opens the door to participate in other water sports, such as canoeing, soiling, water skiing, surfing and wind surfing to name a few. Those with special needs share the same values, and their performances in achieving and enjoying traditional stroke patterns, in swimming distance and in competitive events are outstanding.

Communities not fortunate enough to contain physical rehabilitation facilities, medical facilities or other venues for the disabled may have little access to adapted aquatics programs for people with disabilities. Where and if the demand exists, you may want to start your own adapted aquatics program (Angelo, 1997). Based on the number of disabled participants, the staff should minimally include at least one certified teacher of adapted aquatic, several aides, and a group of dependable volunteers with a background in swimming and life guarding.

Adapted programs work well one on one, but not all programs can afford to incur this cost. However, programs should not have one or two individuals overseeing a large group of disabled participants while they recreate in the water on their own. Adapted aquatic programs should adapt and personalize aquatic skills to the needs of the disabled individuals. Each program, despite budgetary need should strive for the best and they should accept nothing less. Community based aquatic programs can) along with the staff that teach or manage these programs. The success of these programs is dependent upon the imagination, enthusiasm and energy of the aquatic staff. The results are only limited by the staff's drive to better the human condition.

Water is the high tech tool of the nineties (Napoletan, 1995). The protective quality of buoyancy is what brings highly dysfunctional and acute orthopedic patents to the pool. Immersion in the water is dependent upon the condition of the participant and his/her fears in the water. Total immersion, which is about eighty percent of the body under water, is ideal. The very medium that forms this protective environment has the potential to increase muscular strength in all planes of the body. Water resistance can be manipulated in numerous ways. The most common and obvious ones if=s the speed at which one moves the extremities (especially the lower ones) through the water. The length and orientation of the segment being moved also affects the amount of resistance that will be encountered. Paddles, foam dumbbells, flotation belts and webbed gives in addition to other buoyancy and resistance devices can also be utilized to increase the amount of resistance.

Regardless of who the aquatic program is there for, one positive effect is consistently reported among post-surgical patients, individuals with chronic disease, or elite athletes is the psychological benefit. It gives all individuals a tremendous life and a sense of well being. People are fascinated by water. Its colors soothe, its sounds paucity and it temporarily liberates us from the tyranny of gravity (which could be note as the most important) effects all of us. It translates into compliance of the patient, the extremely for the athlete, and lifelong exercise habits for those of us who prefer not to take a beating.

There are no hard and fast rules for designing an aquatic therapy program, which can be seen as a benefit because you can design your own program. The flexibility in water temperature, type of exercise anywhere aquatic exercise fits into a program makes it a workout almost anyone can do. The patients who do the least, for the most part, and move the slowest because of their injuries need to be in warmer water. Water temperatures should vary from 80-90 degrees. Physiological intensity, not just the intensity of muscle contraction, is a factor in temperature. Designing an aquatic therapy program will be dependent upon the individual and his/her goals. You want to design a program that will not aggravate an injury, and one that is going to protect the injury while the rest of the body is kept in shape. Protecting an injury could be taping or bracing it, or it could just be modifying the exercises that the injured area will be utilizing. Aquatic therapy is not only for surgical patients, and it should be included in a regular fitness program. Aquatic therapy should be used as part of a training program to prevent the occurrence of overuse injuries (Trumbull, 1996).

One of the many ways of extending opportunities in aquatics is initiate a competitive swimming program. For individuals who enjoy competition, this type of program gives a great deal of enjoyment and the opportunity to achieve. Many good competitive programs are run on a strictly local level, but there are advantages to being affiliated with a national program. Some of the benefits offered by national organization include materials, grants, consultant services, and greater geographical area of competition. Many different organizations plan and organize athletic and competitive programs for people with specific impairments. These competitions are usually organized so there is competition at every level: local, state, regional, national and international. Some groups are highly organized while other is rather informal.

Competition has both personal and group aspects that involve striving to attain a personally important goal.
- **On a personal level the individual may:**
    - Compete with him to improve his own performance.
    - Try to attain a specific goal: a completion certificate, a ribbon, points, a medal etc.
- **On the group level, the individual has the opportunity to:**
    - Cooperate with other to achieve a mutual goal.
    - Compete with others to win a position on a team or place in a group.

Individual and group competition can provide both the satisfaction of success and the feeling of accomplishment and thus can become highly motivating for individuals of all ages who have a disability. Competition can contribute greatly to the growth and development of disabled individuals, just as it does for those who are not disabled.

- **Some of the benefits are:**
    - The opportunity to participate in increased physical activities.
    - The possibilities for new experiences-traveling, staying overnight away from home, eating in public facilities, meeting celebrities, seeing more of the world, etc.
    - Opportunities to feel important, as an individual of worth and dignity about whom others care.
    - The opportunity to expand social interaction with others who have disabilities and well as with peers who are no disabled.
    - Opportunities to exercise self discipline in a variety of situations.

Despite the potential contribution that athletic programs can make to the life experiences and well being of disabled individuals, the crucial determinant of whether they are positive or negative forces rests with the leaders involved in the program. Careful evaluation must be made to determine the best approach to programming competitive activities for special populations. The guiding criterion must be what does the most good for the greatest number while still meeting each individual's special needs. Some disabled individuals are perfectly capable of participation in competitive programs with the nondisabled peers and will not need nor want special programs. There is a particular need in this country for mainstreaming the adult competitive programs in order to enjoy the competitive experience. Flexibility pf [programming is important to success. Integrated opportunities should be available to individuals when they can safely compete and will achieve personal satisfaction in doing so. Separate programs for individuals who cannot participate in integrated mainstream programs may provide the unique experiences available in competitive opportunities.

The use of small craft in recreation for the disabled is becoming more widespread every year. Camps and institutions for the disabled are beginning to include small craft activities in their programs.

The reasons for the increase in such boating usage include the following:
- Boating activates are enjoyable and provide additional recreational and social experiences.
- With little modification, outboard boating, canoeing, and sailing activities are possible for most people with disabilities.
- Canoeing activities, in particular, can provide needed exercise. Once in the craft. The operation has to do very little moving round; thus people with limited ambulatory skills can obtain exercise.
- The excitement of sailing a boat in the wind or paddling a canoe on a body of water and the opportunity to do something outdoors in the sun can

surely be seen as motivational factors.
- The opportunity to compete with nondisabled individuals and the opportunity to participate in activities with the nondisabled on an equal basis can also be seen as motivational factors

Most small craft enthusiasts recall their first experience in a canoe or a small boat as being almost daring. For those who are capable swimmers, this is an exciting but necessarily alarming experience. For individuals with disabilities, however, certain factors may cause anxiety-inability to see or hear what is happening, for instance. Consequently, it is most desirable that disabled individuals who participate in small craft activities be safe and confident swimmers.

Where the impairment does not significantly lessen the individual's functioning capacity and no adaptations are needed, regular small craft courses may and should be taught. The biggest handicap that most disabled individuals have is the restriction placed up them by society. With initiative, imagination, and patience, small craft courses can be adapted in a safe manner for these individuals. Disabled individuals can be provided with a recreational outlet that has been overlooked all too often in the past and we should not continue this pattern. As with the teaching of swimming, skills may need to be broken down into simple components so that students may readily experience success.

A file should be kept one each adapted aquatic participant, which includes a medical release form indicating the nature of the disability, body parts affected, method of ambulation, prescribed medications and a physician's approval for enrollment in the program. The file should also include an evaluation form designed to measure range of motion of all body parts, as well s strength and endurance. Additional forms should evaluate each person's level of swimming ability and mastery of various aquatic skills. Finally the file should include a class by class entry signed by the teacher or person in charge, describing the process of the participant and what was accomplished in that individual session. Remember, aquatics is the wave of the future.

Chapter 9

∽

QUALITIES TO LOOK FOR IN AN INSTRUCTOR:

- Every water safety or swimming instructor should be trained and certified in first aid and CPR. It is also best for all involved if there is separate lifeguard on duty as the child's safety must be the priority in any class. Children should never be left alone and should be constantly monitored in the aquatastic environment.
- The instructor should want to be teaching and should be happy and enthusiastic as he or she is teaching the class. Patience is also key here as teaching children to swim takes a lot of time and effort. Children need to feel comfortable in their environment and the instructor needs to allow each child develop and progress at his or her own rate.
- Crying does not have to be seen in the class to define a successful lesson. If there are any tears they need to be taken care of and they are usually due to fears in the water or the fear of a new situation or change of environment.
- Younger children should have parents in or near the aquatic environment as this is a good time for bonding. It is not a necessity for the parent to be in the water. I have a tendency to let the parents watch so the child can gain confidence and learn how to be independent. If the parent if interfering with the lesson I will ask him or her to leave so the child can learn how to swim. I will also ask a parent to leave if the lesson cannot be completed with the parent in the area.
- Children should not be forced into a situation until he or she is ready. The best way to gain trust is to tell the child exactly what is going on and hopefully they will trust you enough to try what you want them to do in the water.
- A good instructor needs to know the names and abilities of the children he or she is teaching. Age is a guideline as should be used as such. The classes should be adapted to the child or children according to their ability and not their age as every child develops on his or her own.
- Swimming lessons should be reinforced as often as possible to keep the

child focusing on what needs to be done. The things that were taught in class should the focus of what you work on with your child.
- The parent should be able to talk to the instructor and ask questions to make sure he or she is properly teaching the child. You need to know that your child is happy and properly taken care of in the aquatic environment. The instructor needs to find a way to make the child happy and want to be in that lesson.
- Look at the programs in your area and see what is offered and choose what is best for you. Find something that offers what will help your child learn to swim while maintaining your sanity knowing that your child is safe. Make sure that all of your needs are met as a parent.
- Look at the entire program has to offer but safety should be the key concept taught. Children will become more confident in the aquatastic environment over time and they will also become more aware of their bodies and how they work in the aquatic environment. A child that swims will also learn to become more independent and will learn how to think at an earlier age as he or she becomes a problem solver.
- A child can become fearful or will adapt the aquatic environment all depending on his or her experience in the water. Swimming the aquatastic way should have your child looking forward to swimming lessons and a love for the water and all it has to offer.
- Children's classes need to be taught for the child to learn and understand what is being done. Readiness to learn should be the key. These classes must be taught on the child's level of thinking.
- Children should not want to get out of the water in the aquatastic environment as they are having too much fun. The first lesson sets the tone and will determine if the child will come back for more lessons. You need to teach in a supportive and positive environment. The child can learn best when he or she is happy and enjoying what he or she is doing.

ELEMENTS OF SUCCESSFUL INSTRUCTION

Learning styles are just another way of looking at how people approach ways of learning. There are 3 main types of learning styles; visual learners, auditory learners and tactile/kinesthetic learners. People are usually geared toward learning in one of these 3 approaches, but each individual learner will adjust to his or own learning style. Knowing these 3 areas will help us better teach our students how to swim in the aquatastic environment.

Visual learners need to see the instructor's body language and facial expressions to fully understand what information in contained throughout the lesson. These students tend to prefer sitting at the front of the room in order to avoid visual distractions such as other people's heads. These learners will usually think in pictures and learn best through the use of visual aids such as diagrams, books, overheads, videos and/or handouts. These students need to get everything in detail and their notes will be long with great description. They will need the great detail in order to absorb the information. Visual learners talk sparingly but dislike listening for too long. These people tend to favor words such as see, picture and imagine. Visual learners tend to become distracted by untidiness or movement. These learners also tend to prefer direct, face to face or personal meetings.

Auditory learners will learn best through verbal lectures, discussions and listening to what others have to say. These learners interpret meaning by listening to the tone of voice, pitch and speed. Written information here has little meaning until it is heard. These students will usually benefit from reading the text aloud and using a tape recorder. These people prefer the telephone and easily get distracted by sounds or noises. Auditory learners enjoy listening but are very impatient to talk and they tend to use hear, tune and think.

Tactile/kinesthetic learners will greatly benefit with a hands on approach. These learners actively explore the physical world around him or her. These students usually tend to have a hard time sitting still for long periods and may become distracted as they feel a need for activity and exploration. These people gesture and use expressive movements and use words such as feel, touch and hold. Tactile learners also become and are easily distracted by any activity around him or her. When interacting with this type of learner you will tend to walk or participate in an activity with them.

GETTING READY TO TEACH: SAFETY OF YOUR STUDENTS:

- First priority or concern is for the safety of your students at all times. Do not endanger the safety of your students. Look at your aquatic environment and identify all dangers around you.
- Accidents are caused by personal practices of students or by a condition of the aquatic environment.
- You need to recognize or eliminate hazards to minimize effects if it is eliminated then you do not need to worry about it. But if you recognize it, you will still be aware of it and if there is a need for concern.
- Rules and regulations are much easier to enforce if they are accepted in that particular way or situation. You need to explain your reasons for the rules and regulations.

PRESENTING YOUR TEACHING MATERIAL:

- Your success as an instructor may partially be determined by your ability to communicate with your students.
- Get attention of the students – do not start without their attention focused on you.
- Talk with your students not at them.
- Know what is going on around you.
- Be prepared – know what you are doing ahead of time.

- Be positive and show enthusiasm while teaching.
- Use short, brief, and easy to understand sentences.

TEACHING METHODS:

- Demonstrate exactly what you want done and explain it step by step. Make sure your directions are clear and easy to understand.
- Repetition – do it over and over again. It may get boring but it needs to be done. Perfect practice makes perfect.
- Praise is their reward so make it sincere. Accentuate the positive and ignore the negative and tell them you are proud of them.
- Be on time for lessons. Give your child time to relax, observe other classes and become familiar with your surroundings. Stay calm as children can sense anxiety.
- Safety first, last and always. Children need to learn and develop safe habits in and around any aquatic environment. Children are NOT responsible and have little judgment ability. Never turn your back on the child. You must constantly watch him or her at all times. Teach your child safety rules in and around the aquatic environment.
- Do not over set goals for the child. It is better to reset goals as the child gets older and understands more. Start out small and leave room for them to grow. You need to allow some freedom.
- Give encouragement and be understanding. Be patient and keep trying to give help, love and praise as swimming is one of the hardest things to learn, yet people expect fantastic results with almost no learning time.
- Crying is ok and a part of learning. It should be expected from time to time. Do not get upset over it.
- Do not compare children. Let them progress at a pace that is comfortable to them as all children have different temperaments and personalities.

RONDA BRODSKY'S BIOGRAPHY

Ronda began her professional Aquatic career at the Jewish Community Center in West Bloomfield, Michigan as their first Aquatic Director. She then moved on to Franklin Fitness and Racquet Club in Southfield, Michigan as their first Aquatic Director. While at both facilities she introduced the Hydro-Tone System for Aquatic Exercise. While at those facilities she managed all aspects of the aquatic avenues. This included seeking lifeguard, swimming instructors and aquatic personal trainers. Ronda has spent much time rehabilitating people in the aquatic environment as it is easier and more efficient than land for most people. She has rehabilitated numerous professional athletes after surgeries getting them back to their sport in better condition. Ronda has supervised and trained a great number of lifeguards in her time. At her peek times in the pools she had about 50 lifeguards and swimming instructors under her guidance. Ronda has managed three pools in one facility during the summer seasons. Her experience as a swimming instructor has had her teach over 1000 students. Seeking a more educational based atmosphere, she completed her teaching certification after she had already attained her Masters of Science degree in Physical Education. She is presently a member of the Aquatic Exercise Association where she previously served as an Advisory Board Member. She has presented locally and internationally on Aquatic Emergency Procedures. Ronda is also a frequent contributor to the AKWA letter, an international trade publication. Ronda's Bachelor of Science degree is from Michigan State University in Family Consumer Sciences with an emphasis on children; where she also earned a ZA endorsement. Her Masters degree and her teaching certification in Physical Education and Health were from Eastern Michigan University. Ronda has the following certifications:

- American Council on Exercise Group Fitness Instructor
- American Red Cross AED Instructor
- American Red Cross CPR and First Aid Instructor
- American Red Cross Lifeguarding Instructor
- American Red Cross Water Safety Instructor
- Aquatic Exercise Association Aquatic Fitness Instructor

REFERENCES AND BIBLIOGRAPHY

1. American Red Cross. CPR For the Professional Rescuer. St. Louis, Missouri; Mosby Year Book, 1993.
2. American Red Cross. Lifeguard Training. Washington D.C.; American National Red Cross, 1983.
3. American Red Cross. Swimming and Aquatic Safety. Washington D.C.; American National Red Cross, 1981.
4. Amateur Swimming Association. Anyone Can Swim. Understanding and Coping with Special Needs. Great Britain; Crowood Press, 1989.
5. Angelo, P. & Stewart C. You Can Start Your Own Adapted Aquatics Program. Aquatics International; 9.4, 23-27, 1997.
6. Block, M.E. & Etz, K. The Pocket Reference: A Tool for Fostering Inclusion. Journal of Physical Education, Recreation & Dance; 66, 47-51, 1995.
7. Brisbane, Holly E. The Developing Child. Glencoe/McGraw Hill; Peoria, Illinois, 2000.
8. Clayton, Robert D. & David G. Thomas. Professional Aquatic Management. Champagne, Illinois; Human Kinetics Books, 1989.
9. Gallahue, David L. Understanding Motor Development in Children. John Wiley & Sons Inc., 1982.
10. Haywood, K.M. Lifespan Motor Development. Champagne, Illinois; Human Kinetics Books, 1986.
11. Kinder, Tom & Julie See. Aqua Aerobics – A Scientific Approach. Eddie Bowers Publishing Inc.; Dubuque, Iowa, 1992.
12. Kozub, F.M. & Porretta, D. Athletes with Disabilities. Interscholastic Athletic Benefits for all. Journal of Physical Education, Recreation & Dance; 67, 19-24,1996.
13. Napoletan, J. Diving Into Aquatic Therapy. Biomechanics; II.3, 26-31, 1995.
14. New Games Foundation. More New Games & Playful Ideas. Dolphin Books/Doubleday Collins; Garden City, New York, 1981.
15. Paciorek, M.J. & Jones, J.A. Sports and Recreation for the Disabled. Carmel IN; Cooper Publishing Company, 1994.
16. Rimmer, J.H. Programming for Clients with Disabilities. IDEA Today; 15.5, 26-35,1997.
17. Rink, J.E. Teaching Physical Education for Learning. St. Louis, Missouri; Mosby Year Book, 1985.
18. Sherrill, C. Adapted Physical Activity, Recreation and Sport. WCB

McGraw-Hill; Boston, MA, 1998.
19. Trumbull, J. Water as a Healing Factor. Aquatics International; 8.4, 24-26, 1996.
20. VanDerveer, B.J. Activities and Games for the Disabled in Aquatics. NRPA Aquatic News; Illinois, 1993.
21. Vannier, M. Physical Activities for the Handicapped. Englewood Cliffs; Prentice Hall Inc., 1977.

Aquatics by Sprint
Phone: 800 – 235 - 2156
Email: alex@sprintaquatics.com
Website: www.sprintaquatics.com

Aquatics by Sprint offers you the latest equipment and education for aquatic exercise and therapy rehabilitation. Check our wholesale prices and quality before buying. Our DVDs are reviewed by P.T.s and are an excellent reference tool.

Hydro-Tone Fitness Systems
Phone: 800-622-8663
Email: info@hydrotone.com
Website: www.hydrotone.com

Hydro-Tone produces specially designed and patented resistive aquatic exercise and therapy equipment and floatation belts.

D. K. Douglas Company - The Wet Wrap
Phone: 800 – 334 – 9070
Email: wetwrap@wetwrap.com
Website: www.wetwrap.com

D.K.Douglas Company water wear of neoprene and Lycra will help with your warmth during all your water activities.

Kiefer – Adolf Kiefer and Associates
Phone: 800 – 323 - 4071
Website: www. Kiefer.com
Supplying everything but the water since 1947! If you are in the water, we have what you need - swimwear, fitness and therapy equipment, footwear, accessories and so much more!

These are the main suppliers that I have utilized with great success. Please note there are many more out there.

Aquatic Exercise Association (AEA)
P.O. Box 1609
Nokomis, FL 34274-1609
(888) AEA-WAVE
Fax: (914) 486-8820
Website: www.aeawave.com
**This website is a good source of information if you are interested in getting certified through the AEA or would just like to learn more about their association.

American Swimming Coaches Association (ASCA)
(800) 356-2722
Fax: (954) 563-9813
Website: www.swimmingcoach.org
**Although this website doesn't contain information on aquatic exercise and rehab, it did contain an extensive amount of information on swimming in general. Since this is our aquatics section we thought that this would be appropriate to include. For those of you who are swimming coaches or are interested in more information on how you can improve your swim facility this is an excellent site!

American Red Cross (ARC)
National Headquarters
2025 East Street NW
Washington D.C. 20006
Phone: 202 – 303 – 4498
Website: www.redcross.org

The Red Cross is committed to saving lives and easing suffering. This diverse organization serves humanity and helps you by providing relief to victims of disaster, both locally and globally. The Red Cross is responsible for half of the nation's blood supply and blood products. The Red Cross gives health and safety training to the public and provides emergency social services to U.S. military members and their families. In the wake of an earthquake, tornado, flood, fire, hurricane or other disaster, it provides relief services to communities across the country.

USA Swimming
Among the many services are publications, educational programs, fundraising activities, sports medicine programs, resources and general information about swimming-related activities. The headquarters staff is available to assist you in answering questions or providing general information about USA Swimming
Phone: 719.866.4578
Website: www.usaswimming.org

CPSIA information can be obtained
at www.ICGtesting.com
Printed in the USA
FFOW05n2047180117